AMERICAN ROCK 'N' ROLL

AMERICAN ROCK 'N' ROLL T☆O☆U☆R

DAVE WALKER

THUNDER'S MOUTH PRESS

Published by
Thunder's Mouth Press
54 Greene Street, Suite 4S
New York, NY 10013

LIBRARY OF CONGRESS CATALOGING IN PUBLICATION DATA

Walker, Dave, 1958–
American rock 'n' roll tour / by Dave Walker, —1st ed.
p.   cm.
Includes bibliographical references and index.
ISBN 1-56025-041-0 : $13.95
1. Rock music—United States—History and criticism.   2. United
States—Guidebooks   3. Musical landmarks—United States—
Guidebooks.   I. Title
ML3534.W28   1992
781.66'0973—dc20   92-19994
                                                          CIP
                                                          MN
Portions of the Memphis and Miami sections of this book have previously appeared in the
Phoenix and *Miami New Times*, two metropolitan weekly news magazines. Copyright ©
1987 and 1990, by New Times, Inc. Reprinted by permission.

"(We're an) American Band" copyright © 1972 by Brew Music.
Lyrics reprinted by permission.

Preceding photo is of Woodstock, 1969, © Ken Regan/Camera 5.

Distributed by
Publisher's Group West
4065 Hollis Street
Emeryville, CA 94608
(800) 788-3123

Design and composition by The Sarabande Press
Manufactured in the United States of America

For Judy and Mack and Mom and Dad

Contents

Preface

I t's a little scary to measure the affect rock 'n' roll has had on my life. I'm not a professional musician, don't run a record company, don't work in radio, and I'm not a rock critic. Still, rock 'n' roll music flavors almost everything I've done, everything I do.

Like lots of people, I mark the passage of time by songs. Music triggers my memory more fully than smells, tastes, or touch. And, now that I think of it, most of the pleasure reading I've done is somehow related to music or the music business. I love rock's history, its lore, even some of its trivia. If there is a rhythm to life, mine has a big back beat. This book is the product of all that.

One of the most pleasant discoveries I made during the research is that rock 'n' roll isn't an exclusively coastal phenomenon. The truth is that the music emerged from pockets of creativity all over the map, then radiated to the music capitals, New York and Los Angeles.

Another finding was that rock history has been made in venues beyond sterile recording studios and concert halls. Often, the most important stuff happened in hotel rooms, bars, restaurants, and, sadly, airplane crash sites. In assembling *American Rock 'n' Roll Tour*, I've tried to highlight the sites that have had the greatest impact on rock's history, the places where that history is enshrined, or, in some cases, the places where just plain great rock 'n' roll stuff happened. What I ended up with runs the gamut from the well-known to the obscure, Graceland to Madam Marie's, Woodstock to Altamont; from the biggest cities to the dustiest little dots on the map.

As I discovered on my own tour, too many of these places no longer exist in any form. So, this book is part history, part travelogue, and part petition for the preservation of our cultural heritage, no matter how goofy or out-of-the-way some of the sites may seem. If we don't save landmarks like the Chess Records studio in Chicago, our grandkids are going to be extremely pissed off.

One final note before you start: While a lot of these sites are equipped as tourist attractions, many others are not. The off-limits landmarks may include recording studios, private homes, or places of business that no longer have anything to do with their glory days in rock. The point is to walk where the giants walked (or, in this case, where the giants plugged in and played), but don't extend your quest beyond where it is welcome. Be cool, in other words.

It's time to start your tour. Grab your car keys (or just find a comfortable chair), crank up the soundtrack, and hit the rock road. Have a great trip.

—D.W.
1992

Acknowledgments

The first thing that occurred to me when this idea came up was, *Seek professional help*. So I did. Without the following newspaper and magazine pop-music experts, *American Rock 'n' Roll Tour* would never have left the gate:

Scott Aiges in New Orleans, Gil Asakawa in Denver, Robert Baird in Phoenix, Greg Baker in Miami, Jeff Bahr in Omaha, Jon Bream in Minneapolis, Thor Christensen in Milwaukee, Charles Cross in Seattle, Mark de la Vina in Philadelphia, Bill DeYoung in Gainesville, Bill Eichenberger in Columbus, Karen Freeman in McComb, Blair Jackson in San Francisco, Don Jacobs in Port Arthur, Dan Matthews in Athens, Don McLeese in Austin, Steve Morse in Boston, Claudia Perry in Houston, Mike Weatherford in Las Vegas, Susan Whitall in Detroit, and Bill Wyman in Chicago.

Also helpful were hundreds of folks in and out of the music business, who either let me interview them, sent me correspondence, or just plain showed me a good time. I'm grateful to all (super-helpers get an exclamation point!). Thanks to: Ric Addy, Brooks Arthur, Harvey Beller, Hal Blaine(!), Martha Blue, Kenny Bosak (!), Owen Bradley, Nathaniel Brewster, Mary Campbell, Dick Clark, Bruce Christensen (!), Charles Conrad, Guy Costa, Jack Curtis, Jerry Dennon, Tom Dowd (!), Joe Edwards, Mickey Elfenbein, Rick Faucher (!), Nathalie Fausty, Barry Fey, Gino Francesconi, Don Frey, Terry Galvin, Lillie Gonzalez, Kay Grinter, Frank Guida, Roger Hawkins, Chuck Haddix, Cal Harris, Jesse Ishikawa, Quinn Ivy, Joe Jorgensen, Bert Kaufman, Ian Kimmet, Dick LaPalma, Don Law, Joel Levy, Bill Ludwig, Jr., Bob Lyndall, Howell J. Malham, Jr. (!), Cosimo Matassa, Huey P. Meaux, Jay Messina, Mike Mitchell, Casey Monahan, Robert Mars, Buck Munger, Heather Nash, James Olness, Michael Olszewski, Sonny Payne, Paul Petraitis, Floyd Ramsey, Brian Ritchie, John Rosenfield, Steve Routhier, Nelson Ruiz, Tim Samuelson, Calris Sayadian,

Peter Schivarelli, Danny Sessums, Dick Sherman, Gerald Sims, Bob Skye, Gary Smith, Richard Smith, Deborah Staley, Bruce Swedien, Joe Tarsia, Bruce Tomaso, Roberta Ulloa (!), Bob Walters, Gary Wojtas, R. Martin Willett (!), and the telephone-reference librarians of America (!!). Sorry if I've left anybody out.

Many of the current and former writers, editors, executives, and support staff at *New Times* in Phoenix are good friends and/or positive professional influences. Thank you, Bob Boze Bell, David Bodney, Deborah Block, Jana Bommersbach, Bart Bull, Michael Burkett, Deborah Cox, Anna Dooling, Heidi Ewart, Rick Feldmann, Tom Fitzpatrick, Terry Greene, Ward Harkavy, Mike Ives, Deborah Laake, Mike Lacey, Jim Larkin, Janice LaRue, Kendra Leon, Scott Spear, Mike Tulumello, Andy Van De Voorde, Sarah Wallace, and Julie Wodzinski.

Jim Mullin, editor at *New Times* in Miami, gave the go-ahead to the article that eventually became this book. So it's really his fault. Also implicated is Scottsdale author and golfing fool Paul Perry, who helped polish and sell the proposal. Totally without fault are Tarah Rider Berry, who did all of my photographic lab work, and Mary Rader, who conjured up the maps.

For still-unknown reasons, Thunder's Mouth publisher Neil Ortenberg thought this crackpot concept might make a book. Marian Cole, also at Thunder's Mouth, was the idea's chief advocate from the beginning, and helped at every step. With luck, their careers will survive it. Editors Donna Jensen and Joan Fucillo worked miracles.

Friends and family to thank include: Paul Rubin, Bev Rubin, Kim MacEachern, Paula Blankenship, John Fitzpatrick, Mark Jennings, Doug MacEachern, Melanie MacEachern, Bev Walker, Charlie Walker, Vera Walker, Bobbie Trower, Bill Trower, and Lucile Trower. These people always seem to be around when I have the most fun.

No matter how much you paid for your copy of this book, Judy and Mack Walker paid more. Their love and support is immeasurable.

THE EAST

CONNECTICUT

New Haven

■ THE NEW HAVEN ARENA

State and Grove Streets, New Haven

The New Haven Arena was one of several Jim Morrison arrest sites around the country. On December 9, 1967, Morrison was necking with a groupie in a backstage shower room when a law-enforcement official approached and gave the couple a hard time. The star got lippy and the officer maced him. Performing later, Morrison used the instrumental break of "Back Door Man" to express his displeasure with the local authorities. He was arrested onstage.

The arena was torn down around 1970, and is now a parking lot for the local phone company.

DELAWARE

Dover

■ CARL PERKINS CRASH SITE

Route 13, Between Dover and Woodside

On March 22, 1956, "Blue Suede Shoes" was on its way to number two on the charts, and Carl Perkins was on his way up from Memphis to tape Perry Como's TV show in New York City. Perkins and his band were traveling by car, with manager Stuart Pinkham at the wheel. A mile north of Woodside, at 6:40 A.M. (they'd been driving all night), the car struck the rear of a truck heading in the same direction, and both vehicles went spinning out of control. The driver of the truck was killed in the wreck; Perkins' brother Jay died later. Perkins was seriously injured, and spent the next six months in the hospital. His career never recovered from the layoff.

MASSACHUSETTS

Boston

■ THE BOSTON ARENA

St. Botolph Street, Boston

The Boston (since renamed Matthews) Arena is on the campus of North-eastern University and is notable for two concert events: In May 1958 a riot broke out there after a "package" show put together by popular disc jockey Alan Freed. The local district attorney filed charges against Freed (he was the only one charged) under an anti-anarchy statute. To make matters worse, Freed became furious with his station, WINS in New York, for failing to stand behind him, and quit. Senate payola investigators went gunning for Freed the next year, but some rock historians point to this concert as the beginning of his end.

A few years later, on November 2, 1962, the first performance of the first Motortown Revue, a traveling cavalcade of Motown stars, was held at the Arena. The acts included the Marvelettes, Mary Wells, the Contours, Marvin Gaye, and the Supremes. Traveling in one bus and several trailing cars, the troupe of 45 singers, musicians, and support personnel went on to play twenty more cities.

The Boston Arena was built in 1910 and has been Northeastern's main athletic facility since the late Seventies. Concerts are still occasionally booked there.

■ THE HARD ROCK CAFE
---

131 Clarendon Street, Boston

The star at the Boston Hard Rock is the hand-painted silk jacket Jimi Hendrix wore at the Monterey Pop Festival and on the *Are You Experienced?* and *Electric Ladyland* album covers. Described by the Hard Rock as "perhaps the greatest single piece of Hendrix iconography in existence," the jacket is displayed flanked by the nineteenth-century, carved wooden gilt angels that hung above Hendrix's bed in London.

Also on display is a double-necked bass guitar from Leland Sklar, who's played behind James Taylor, Jackson Browne, and Phil Collins, among others.

Call 617-424-7625 for hours and information. Also, keep in mind that memorabilia is sometimes rotated from Hard Rock to Hard Rock.

■ THE TEA PARTY

53 Berkeley and 15 Lansdowne Streets, Boston

The Tea Party's first location—famous as one of the leading psychedelic ballrooms in the country—was a converted church that could hold about 700 people. The space featured broad, high walls onto which light shows were projected. The words "Praise Ye the Lord" were inscribed above the stage, and bands had to make their way through the audience to reach it. Led Zeppelin played a four-hour show here (with seven encores) on the group's first American tour, and WBCN, Boston's fabled underground station, once broadcast from a room behind the stage.

The second location was larger—capacity about 1,400—and built into the ground floor of a converted warehouse. Elton John's first American tour brought him here directly after his debut shows at the Troubadour in Los Angeles.

The old church has been divided up and is used for a variety of commercial endeavors. The second Tea Party went through several names and is now known as Avalon. Tea Party Concerts, one of the Northeast's leading promoters, still books shows into the room. Kiss and Ziggy Marley have appeared here, and the space is a favorite of Prince's. The phone number is 617-262-2424.

Cambridge

■ FORT APACHE STUDIO

1 Camp Street, Cambridge

The Fort Apache studio doesn't fit the definition of "rock landmark" yet, but with the discography it's building, it one day just might. The studio opened in the mid-Eighties to serve local alternative rock bands, and has played host to the Pixies, Throwing Muses, Dinosaur Jr., Treat Her Right, Big Dipper, Blake Babies, Buffalo Tom, the Lemonheads, the Connells, and Billy Bragg.

■ HARVARD SQUARE THEATER

10 Church Street, Cambridge

Jon Landau, rock critic for *The Real Paper,* attended a concert here on May 9, 1974, and wrote: "I saw rock and roll future and its name is Bruce Springsteen."

Now called Loew's Harvard Square Theater, the building has been converted into a five-screen movie house. The interior is drastically altered, of course, and nothing much remains from the old place. The phone number for show times is 617-864-4580.

Housatonic

■ THE CHURCH

4 Van Deusenville Road, Housatonic

Arlo Guthrie created a monster when he took out the trash for his friend Alice in 1965. "Alice's Restaurant," the eighteen-minute counterculture anthem, was inspired by Guthrie's arrest for littering on that garbage run.

The Church in Housatonic played a role in the story that became the song, and today it's the headquarters for Guthrie's nonprofit foundation (which sponsors music therapy programs for abused children and assists victims of AIDS), as well as the business office for his mail-order record company, Rising Sun.

The Church offers directions and maps so visitors can follow Guthrie's "Garbage Trail" through neighboring Stockbridge—from Alice's Restaurant to the police station, the Stockbridge Town Dump, and other points of interest.

Van Deusenville Road is located east of Route 183, one of the main north-south courses through the area. Call 413-623-8925 for directions and more information.

Quincy

■ THE ZILDJIAN FACTORY

39 Fayette Street, Quincy

From the Depression through the early Seventies, most of the world's greatest drummers got their cymbals from the Zildjian Factory. The company predates rock (the modern cymbal-making technique was discovered in the seventeenth century and passed down as a family secret until Avedis Zildjian opened his American plant in 1929), but so what?

The company moved to a large, modern plant in Norwall, Massachusetts, during the Seventies.

NEW JERSEY

Cherry Hill

■ THE LATIN CASINO

2235 Marlton Pike, Cherry Hill

A big, flashy nightclub across the river from Philadelphia, the Latin Casino specialized in Vegas-style entertainment, including Frank Sinatra and Diana Ross. But, sadly, the club was made obsolete when star entertainers began to bypass Cherry Hill in favor of the gambling casinos in Atlantic City, an hour to the southeast. The site holds one special memory: it was here that Jackie Wilson had a heart attack during a performance on September 25, 1975. He suffered brain damage as a result of the attack and lapsed into a coma from which he never recovered. Wilson died in January 1984.

At the end of its life, the Latin Casino was converted into a popular disco. But the building was eventually demolished, and a Japanese auto manufacturer has erected an office building on the site.

The Jersey Shore: Where the Atlantic Meets America

For fans of Bruce Springsteen, coastal New Jersey is the Promised Land. From this area's grungy clubs the Boss went on to unimaginable greatness. His roots here are much celebrated in his music and the writings of his fans.

Freehold, where Springsteen was raised (it's supposedly the subject of the sad "My Hometown"), and Asbury Park, the faded oceanside resort from which he launched his career, are the key settings in Springsteen's early-life story, but there are several important stops in this part of the Boss' world.

■ **E STREET, BELMAR**

David Sancious played keyboards in an early version of Bruce Springsteen's band. His mother lived on E Street in Belmar, just south of Asbury Park along the shore. E is a one-way street, running just a few blocks east of Highway 71, the main route into and out of town.

■ **HIGHWAY 9**

Highway 9 (known to New Jersey highway authorities as Route 9) is a major artery through north-central Jersey and is mentioned in the Springsteen anthem "Born to Run." To get there, drive west from Asbury Park along Highway 30. Route 9 runs north from Freehold toward the bright lights of New York.

■ **MADAM MARIE'S**
Fourth Avenue and Boardwalk, Asbury Park

Fortuneteller Madam Marie is mentioned in the Springsteen song, "Fourth of July, Asbury Park (Sandy)." Her stand—a shack planted on the boardwalk a few feet from the Jersey Shore—is one of the last remnants of the era Springsteen memorialized in his early records.

■ **THE STONE PONY**
913 Ocean Avenue, Asbury Park

The Stone Pony closed abruptly in late 1991, but only after building a rich legacy as a Shore-scene clubhouse. Even after all its neighbors on Asbury Park's

E Street, Belmar, New Jersey

seafront had passed on, the place remained viable for years, due entirely to Springsteen's propensity to show up and jam with whoever was playing there. He stopped by often during the Seventies and Eighties, and fans packed the house in hopes of catching sight of the otherwise reclusive Boss. Perhaps the final document of the Pony's great run will be the video for the Southside Johnny and the Asbury Jukes song, "It's Been a Long Time," which was filmed here a few days before the clubhouse closed. Bruce, Southside Johnny Lyon, Little Steven Van Zandt (who called himself Miami Steve when he played guitar in the E Street Band), and Jon Bon Jovi all took the stage for one last time. If the Stone Pony is still closed when you read this, a grand era has definitely passed.

Morris Plains

■ GREYSTONE HOSPITAL

West Hanover Avenue, outside Morris Plains

One of the reasons Bob Dylan left Minnesota and came to New York was to find Woody Guthrie. Guthrie was suffering from advanced hereditary Huntington's Chorea, and he'd been picked up for vagrancy and committed to Greystone in May 1956. Dylan found him here in January 1961.

During this same period, Dylan also arrived unannounced one day at the Guthrie family home in Queens, New York. Woody's wife, Marjorie, was at work, and Dylan talked his way past the baby-sitter and met the Guthrie children, including teenage son Arlo.

Now called Greystone Park Psychiatric Hospital, the facility is located about an hour's drive from New York City. Go west on Route 80 to exit 42, which takes you down Route 202 south to Morris Plains. There are signs for the hospital in town. The phone number is 201-538-1800.

West Orange

■ THE HOUSE OF MUSIC

1400 Pleasant Valley Way

The House of Music is a typically successful recording studio with a typically impressive client list—Eric Clapton, Keith Richards, Southside Johnny and the Asbury Jukes, Yngwie Malmsteen, Joe Cocker, John Mayall, Patti Smith, Curtis Blow, Jimmy Cliff, Cinderella, Warrant, and the Fabulous Thunderbirds have all recorded here. Meat Loaf made *Bat Out of Hell,* and Kool and the Gang recorded and mixed most of their biggest hits (including the anthem "Celebration") at the House. The studio also mixed the album with the best title in all of heavy metal: Warrant's *Dirty Rotten Filthy Stinking Rich.*

West Orange

■ THE EDISON NATIONAL HISTORIC SITE

Main Street and Lakeside Avenue

Thomas Edison actually invented the phonograph somewhere else, but he polished the idea at his home in West Orange and it's by far the best place to get the big picture on perhaps the greatest American inventor.

Take Bus 66 from the Port Authority Terminal in New York City, or drive west on Interstate 280 to Exit 10; go right on Northfield, then left on Main.

NEW YORK

Bearsville

■ BEARSVILLE STUDIOS

Route 212 and Wittenberg Road, Bearsville

Albert Grossman, Bob Dylan's manager, founded Bearsville in 1971; Grossman's wife has been in charge since his death in the mid-Eighties. Bearsville is a favorite spot for those seeking a respite from big-city distractions, and among its many charms are the attached residences—artists can move right in until a project is complete.

Such artists have included the Isley Brothers, Dr. John, Simple Minds, Psychedelic Furs, Cinderella, Tesla, R.E.M., Robbie Robertson, Cher, the Pretenders, Suzanne Vega, and Megadeth. The Rolling Stones rehearsed in Studio A for six weeks prior to their 1979 American tour. Producer Bob Clearmountain brings a lot of his projects here, too.

The Band's *Cahoots* album, recorded at Bearsville, is said to be an aural representation of the local atmosphere, as is all of the music that Todd Rundgren has made here.

Bethel

■ THE WOODSTOCK MUSIC AND ART FAIR SITE

Hurd and West Shore Roads, outside Bethel

Woodstock was a watershed event, still remembered fondly as the greatest and the most peaceful, dynamic, and mellow gathering of musical youth ever. It was also muddy, uncomfortable, unsanitary, and drug-ridden. It was, in other words, the Sixties incarnate.

The dates were August 15, 16, and 17, 1969. Festival tickets sold for $18, but ended up functioning only as souvenirs: the sheer number of attendees and gate crashers forced the promoters to declare Woodstock a "free" concert.

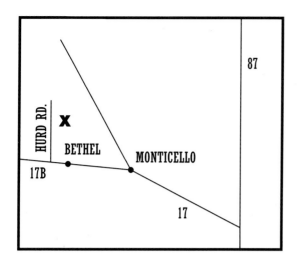

The Woodstock site

Ultimately, the crowd was half a million strong. Traffic was so backed up during the festival that the New York Thruway had to be closed. The weather was nasty—alternating between hard rain, high wind, and melting heat—and the entire festival site was declared a national disaster area.

The popular movie about Woodstock did not show any of the backstage bickering, post-festival heavyweight music-business maneuvering, or drug-dosing (members of the Who claim they were tripping against their will onstage), and it also left several acts on the cutting room floor—including The Band, the Grateful Dead, and Creedence Clearwater Revival.

In another sin of omission, most of the crowd went home before Jimi Hendrix (the festival's highest-paid performer, at $18,000) started playing on Monday morning.

The near-Bethel location was actually the festival's third setting. The promoters had negotiated with Woodstock and Wallkill, but those towns turned them down. The site can be reached by driving north on Hurd Road off Route 17B. To get to 17B, drive west from the New York Thruway on Highway 17. The turn for 17B comes up just as you pass through Monticello.

Once in Bethel, the key landmark is the Bethel Country Store, an old structure on the north side of the road; the Hurd Road turnoff is a quarter-mile beyond the store (a white farmhouse stands on the south side of the road at the intersection). Drive up Hurd Road until you come to West Shore Road.

A concrete marker, placed approximately where the stage stood, lists the performers who played at Woodstock. It also carries a metal plaque of the

Flower children at Woodstock

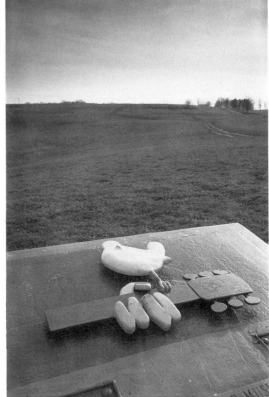

*Monument to the Woodstock
Generation
(Bethel, New York)*

Woodstock logo—the little bird perched on a guitar. Fans typically leave personal offerings (cigarette butts, bottle caps, etc.) to the memory of hippie paradise.

■ PERFORMERS AT WOODSTOCK

Joan Baez	The Jefferson Airplane
The Band	Janis Joplin
Blood, Sweat, and Tears	Melanie
The Paul Butterfield Blues Band	Mountain
Canned Heat	Quill
Joe Cocker	Santana
Country Joe and the Fish	John Sebastian
Creedence Clearwater Revival	Sha Na Na
Crosby, Stills, and Nash	Ravi Shankar
The Grateful Dead	Sly and the Family Stone
Arlo Guthrie	Bert Sommer
Tim Hardin	Sweetwater
Richie Havens	Ten Years After
Jimi Hendrix	The Who
The Incredible String Band	Johnny Winter

Blauvelt

■ 914 SOUND STUDIOS

34 Route 303, Blauvelt

The 914 studio (named for the local area code) was small and only operated for a few years in the Seventies, but it made history anyway. Blood, Sweat, and Tears recorded here, as did Melanie, Janis Ian (*Between the Lines*), and others. But the studio's most famous as the recording site of Bruce Springsteen's first two albums (*Greetings From Asbury Park* and *The Wild, the Innocent and the E Street Shuffle*), plus the song "Born to Run." Bruce and the E Streeters were regulars at the Blauvelt Coach Diner, which still operates next door.

The building most recently housed a meat company (when the studio took over, it had been an old auto-repair garage). Currently, it's empty.

Hartsdale

■ ALAN FREED'S GRAVE

Ferncliff Cemetery, Secor Road, Hartsdale

Freed's ashes have been kept in a crypt here since his death in the mid-Sixties. He wasn't the father of rock 'n' roll, just its rowdy uncle.

Hartsdale is a suburb of New York City. Take the New York Thruway to Saw Mill River Road, then exit at Secor Road. The cemetery's number is 914-693-4700.

New York

■ A & R STUDIOS

12 West 48th Street, 799 Seventh Avenue, 322 West 48th Street, New York

A & R was hot for a couple of decades, and in addition to a parade of recording work for television and radio commercials, film scores, and classical and jazz albums, the studio produced much great rock 'n' roll. For a long time, producer Phil Ramone used A & R as his home base, and helped Paul Simon and Billy Joel make some of their best music. Bob Dylan recorded early sessions for *Blood on the Tracks* in these studios in September 1974, before leaving for Minneapolis to complete (and, in some cases, rerecord) some cuts. The proto-punk guitarists from the band Television recorded *Marquee Moon* at A & R in November 1976.

Jim and Andy's, a bar on the corner of 48th Street and Sixth Avenue (just downstairs from A & R), was a popular hangout for musicians and recording technicians from all over town.

Today, though, none of the addresses remain as they were during A & R's heyday.

253 West 125th Street, New York

The Apollo Theater was built in 1913, became a burlesque house for a while, and achieved shrinehood in the Thirties. The two balconies, the Amateur Nights, the Flames—all are famous. Of course, the greatest black performers have played here, including . . . well, all of them.

A few rock 'n' roll moments:

- Smokey Robinson wrote "My Girl" backstage at the Apollo with Ronnie White. Before coming off the road to record the tune, Smokey rehearsed it with the Temptations during breaks.
- The greatest live record of all time was made here—*The James Brown Show Live at the Apollo '62.* It stayed on the charts for 66 weeks.
- Buddy Holly and the Crickets performed here in 1957, during a short tour of predominantly black theaters.

The Apollo, which has closed and reopened a few times in its history (a $6 million renovation was done in the mid-Eighties), at press time was facing new challenges. Call 212-749-5838 to check on its status.

■ **ATLANTIC RECORDS**

234 West 56th Street, 11 West 60th Street, 1841 Broadway, New York

Atlantic Records, perhaps the greatest of the independent labels, was founded in 1948 by Ahmet Ertegun, Nesuhi Ertegun, and Herb Abramson. Initially the company recorded jazz, but soon it moved to classic rhythm and blues. The Drifters, the Coasters, Ray Charles, and Aretha Franklin all worked for Atlantic. Later, so did the Rolling Stones, Led Zeppelin, and Cream.

The West 56th Street address was an old carriage house, five stories tall with a skylight on the top floor where the studio was. By day the space held desks and busy executives; at night, the owners pushed the furniture to the walls and made recordings. According to Tom Dowd, Atlantic engineer and

The Apollo Theatre

producer, most of Ray Charles' Atlantic hits (including "What'd I Say") were done in this studio, as were Coasters classics ("Yakety Yak," "Poison Ivy," "Charlie Brown") and Bobby Darin's "Splish-Splash." Jerry Wexler was another top Atlantic producer, who helped Wilson Pickett and Aretha Franklin develop some of their hits.

Atlantic moved in 1960 to adjacent buildings near Columbus Circle and built Studio A into the second floor of 11 West 60th Street. Here, Ben E. King's "Stand By Me," Franklin's "Respect," various songs by the Young Rascals, Cream's *Disraeli Gears,* and the Velvet Underground's *Loaded* were recorded.

Atlantic still keeps offices in some of its space in the Broadway building, but the studio closed in the late Eighties.

■ THE BITTER END

147 Bleecker Street, New York

One of a handful of legendary Greenwich Village clubs, The Bitter End became famous in the Sixties for its comedy (Woody Allen, Bill Cosby, Richard Pryor, and Joan Rivers played here in their standup days) and for folk music. The club booked Peter, Paul, and Mary for a solid year.

Neil Young, James Taylor, Carly Simon, and Arlo Guthrie all took significant career steps following engagements at The Bitter End; in 1973, Peter Asher saw Linda Ronstadt perform here and decided he wanted to manage her.

The show still goes on. Call 212-673-7030 for more information.

■ THE BOTTOM LINE

15 West 4th Street, New York

Since opening night in February 1974 the 400-seat Bottom Line has been popular with music-industry big shots and the New York media. The club's specialty is breakthroughs: Bruce Springsteen first caught the attention of the national press during his five-night stand here in August 1975. Five thousand people saw those ten shows, and thousands more heard a live radio broadcast on the third night. These were the performances that prompted the simultaneous *Time* and *Newsweek* covers.

Ten years after Springsteen's Bottom Line epiphany, a little-known folk singer named Suzanne Vega broke out of obscurity during her eight-show engagement here.

Other artists who have performed on the Bottom Line's stage include Dr. John, Elvis Costello, the Talking Heads, Lou Reed, Edie Brickell and the New Bohemians, Bruce Hornsby and the Range, James Taylor, Miles Davis, and Muddy Waters. Tickets usually start at about $15, and the phone number is 212-228-6300.

■ THE BRILL BUILDING

1619 Broadway, New York

The Brill Building is symbolic of the professional approach to rock 'n' roll songwriting, a tradition that dates back to Tin Pan Alley and the earliest days of American popular music. Dozens of names have been linked with this address. Some of those who have rented offices here:

- Jerry Leiber and Mike Stoller. They wrote many hits for Elvis, and were one of the great songwriting teams.
- Phil Spector. Leiber and Stoller introduced Spector around the Brill Building. (They thought the teenager showed promise.)
- Tony Orlando of Dawn fame. He got his start here as a singer on demo records.
- Doc Pomus and Mort Shuman. Among their songs are "Save the Last Dance for Me," "This Magic Moment," "Little Sister," and "Viva Las Vegas."
- Aldon Music. Entrepreneurs Al Nevins and Don Kirshner launched Aldon, a publishing company, in 1958, and assembled a phenomenally talented writing staff: Neil Sedaka, Howard Greenfield, Barry Mann, Cynthia Weil, Gerry Goffin, and Carole King all were employees, and wrote such hits as "The Loco-Motion," "One Fine Day," "Up on the Roof," "Kicks," "Hungry," and "Will You Still Love Me Tomorrow?"

- Donald Fagen and Walter Becker. They'd later move on to form their own group, Steely Dan, but right out of college they tried to work as pop songwriters.
- Neil Diamond was a Brill Building writer, too, before venturing off as a performer.

The Brill is still an office building, and still has some music-maker tenants.

■ THE BROOKLYN PARAMOUNT

University Plaza, Flatbush Avenue Extension and DeKalb Avenue, Brooklyn

According to one reference source, Chuck Berry first did his duck walk across the Brooklyn Paramount's stage. The theater was also a favorite package-show venue for Alan Freed. During the Easter season of 1958, Freed assembled a lineup that included Berry, who was getting top billing in those days, and Jerry Lee Lewis, at the time rock's hottest performer. Predictably, Berry and Lewis had a dispute over who should close the show. Berry won out, but Jerry Lee finished his penultimate set by whipping out a Coke bottle full of gasoline and torching the piano—while he played it. The dispute was resolved.

The Paramount has been converted into a gym for the Brooklyn campus of Long Island University, but many elements of the theater's interior decor (not to mention the huge pipe organ) are still visible. The university grounds, however, are not open to the public.

■ CAFE BIZARRE

106 West 3rd Street, New York

In the Fifties, Cafe Bizarre's dimly lit air was filled with bongo music, Beat poetry, and the smoke of 10,000 eccentric cigarettes. In the Sixties, the Velvet Underground played here; in the Seventies, standup comics did.

In the Eighties, the building was torn down. A dormitory for the NYU Law School now occupies the site.

Brooklyn Paramount

■ CAFE WHA?

115 MacDougal Street, New York

A folk club and early Bob Dylan haunt, Cafe Wha? will probably be best remembered as the place where Animals bassist Chas Chandler "discovered" Jimi Hendrix, in September 1966. At Chandler's urging, Hendrix moved to England, and there his career began to take off.

Call 212-254-3630 for information.

■ CARNEGIE HALL

881 Seventh Avenue, New York

Everyone wants to play Carnegie Hall at one time or another. The list of pop and rock stars who have done so includes Chicago, T. Rex, Led Zeppelin, the Beatles, Bob Dylan, the Rolling Stones, the Kinks, Hot Tuna, the James Gang, Van Morrison, the Allman Brothers Band, the Dave Clark Five, the Byrds, Elton John, the Doobie Brothers, Pink Floyd, the Rascals, John Mellencamp, Ike and Tina Turner, Ray Charles, Delaney and Bonnie and Friends, the Chambers Brothers, Bill Haley, Chuck Berry, the Four Seasons, Jerry Lee Lewis, the Beach Boys, the Jeff Beck Group, Jerry Jeff Walker, Smokey Robinson, the Mothers of Invention, Quicksilver Messenger Service, Neil Young, B. B. King, Billy Joel, Arlo Guthrie, and the Mamas and the Papas. Surprised?

The first rock 'n' roll concert here was a Bill Haley and the Comets show in May 1955. Also on the bill were the McGuire Sisters, Les Paul and Mary Ford, Clifford Brown, and Max Roach. On February 12, 1964, three days after their first appearance on "The Ed Sullivan Show," the Beatles played two concerts at Carnegie Hall. The room was overbooked, so 200 lucky fans got to sit onstage with the band.

Bob Dylan's debut here was less than auspicious. He played in Carnegie's small side room, Chapter Hall, in November 1961. He drew sixty people and the show lost money.

Building tours are offered three times a day on Mondays, Tuesdays, and Thursdays. Call 212-903-9790 for details.

The Beatles leaving Carnegie Hall after their debut—February 12, 1964

315 Bowery, New York

Dump of dumps, CBGB-OMFUG was the mid-Seventies hatchery of the American punk (and later, new wave) movements. In previous lives it had been a wino bar (popular also with members of New York's division of the Hell's Angels) and a country lounge featuring live music in the mornings. Owner Hilly Kristal installed rock 'n' roll in 1974 and then began booking such acts as the Ramones, Blondie, Television, Patti Smith, Talking Heads, the Dead Boys, Wayne County, Mink DeVille, the Dictators, Steve Forbert, Tuff Darts, and the Plasmatics.

CBGB-OMFUG (which stands for Country, Blue Grass, Blues, and Other Music For Uplifting Gourmandisers, or something like that) remains one of New York's best rock venues; the room is long, narrow, dark, and loud, and serves up live music every night. The phone number is 212-982-4052.

■ THE CHELSEA HOTEL

222 West 23rd Street, New York

The Chelsea was built in the 1880s as a co-op apartment building but it has been a hotel since 1905. From the beginning, it's served as a haven for artists, writers, and musicians: Mark Twain, Arthur Miller, O. Henry, Thomas Wolfe, Eugene O'Neill, Tennessee Williams, Nelson Algren, Jimi Hendrix, Janis Joplin, the Grateful Dead, the Mamas and the Papas, the Jefferson Airplane, Jackson Pollock, Willem de Kooning, Larry Rivers, and various members of the Warhol crowd have stayed here.

While in residence, Arthur C. Clarke wrote the screenplay for *2001: A Space Odyssey*, William S. Burroughs wrote *Naked Lunch,* and Bob Dylan composed "Sad-Eyed Lady of the Lowlands."

Dylan Thomas stayed at the Chelsea during a lecture tour in 1953; he left the hotel one night and embarked on what would be a fatal bender. Twenty-five years later, Nancy Spungen was murdered at the hotel. Sex Pistol Sid Vicious was charged with the crime, but died of a heroin overdose before a trial could be held.

For reservations, call 212-243-3700.

CBGBs—the birthplace of American punk (New York City)

■ CHUNG KING STUDIOS

247 Centre Street, New York

In 1985, rappers Run-DMC approached Aerosmith about covering the rockers' song "Walk This Way." Aerosmith did Run-DMC one better, suggesting that the two groups collaborate on the record. So they did, at the Chung King Studios, and the resulting crossover hit boosted Run-DMC and sparked a comeback for Aerosmith.

■ COASTAL TIMES SQUARE

80 West 40th Street, New York

The Coastal Times Square studio was once a penthouse apartment, home to William Randolph Hearst and Marion Davies. The space's most famous occupants in its studio incarnation were probably Jerry Leiber and Mike Stoller, whose March 6, 1959, session here with the Drifters produced "There Goes My Baby."

Today the studio, too, is gone.

■ COLUMBIA STUDIOS

49 East 52nd Street, 207 East 30th Street, 199 Seventh Avenue, New York

During the years it kept its own recording facilities, Columbia worked out of three Manhattan addresses.

The company designated the 30th Street studio, built into an early-nineteenth-century church, for classical music, Broadway cast albums, and selected jazz and pop recordings. Many of Simon and Garfunkel's songs were taped here. The studio operated from the Forties until 1983.

Bob Dylan used the 49 East 52nd Street studios to record *The Freewheelin' Bob Dylan, The Times They Are A-Changin', Another Side of Bob Dylan, Bringing It All Back Home*, and *Highway 61 Revisited*. Miles Davis recorded *Bitches Brew* in the second-floor Studio B here in August 1969.

The Seventh Avenue studio (taken over from A & R, which had built the room in 1967), had a stairwell with a reputation for fabulous echo effects.

Bob Dylan at an early recording session, Columbia Studios (New York City)

Columbia talent magnet John Hammond, who played a crucial role in the careers of Billie Holiday, Count Basie, Benny Goodman, Aretha Franklin, Bob Dylan, Bruce Springsteen, and Stevie Ray Vaughan, could frequently be spotted at the pinball machines in Paramount Drugs on the building's ground floor.

No recording is done in the Columbia studios anymore, although they still function for mastering and editing. The space at 52nd Street houses offices and the Columbia archives. The studios at 30th Street and Seventh Avenue were razed and replaced by high rises.

■ THE DAKOTA

1 West 72nd Street, New York

Built in 1884, the Dakota was New York's first luxury apartment building, the home of Boris Karloff, the setting for *Rosemary's Baby,* and (for most of the Seventies) the residence of John Lennon and Yoko Ono. Mark David Chapman shot and killed Lennon here on December 8, 1980. It happened on the sidewalk near the guard stand at the building's 72nd Street entrance.

■ THE DELMONICO HOTEL

502 Park Avenue, New York

The posh Delmonico witnessed two important events in Beatles history. Late in 1963, Brian Epstein arrived to meet with Ed Sullivan, who lived at the hotel, and negotiated the group's first appearance on Sullivan's TV show. The next year, on August 28, 1964, during the New York stop of their first full tour of America, Bob Dylan introduced the Beatles to marijuana. The boys were no strangers to altered consciousness—having exploited pep pills and Scotch for years—but they'd never tried pot. Dylan was surprised. He'd been hearing "I get high" every time the Beatles sang "I can't hide" in "I Want to Hold Your Hand."

To make your reservation, call 212-355-2500.

The Dakota (New York City)

1697 Broadway, New York

On the night of February 9, 1964, the Beatles changed the world from the soundstage of the Ed Sullivan Theater: more than 73 million people, the largest television audience in history, tuned in to Sullivan's show to see the band play "All My Loving," "Till There Was You," "She Loves You," "I Saw Her Standing There," and "I Want to Hold Your Hand." Clocked at thirteen and a half minutes, the performance was one of the most thrilling in TV history.

The Beatles had never been in New York before. They checked into the Plaza Hotel, which immediately became a disaster area thanks to swarms of teenage fans. The group was cloistered in the hotel's ten-room presidential suite (on the twelfth floor overlooking West 58th Street) but they did manage to sneak out for one night of fun, touring New York's Playboy Club and the Peppermint Lounge.

CBS canceled Sullivan's show in 1971, but not before he brought hundreds of great acts—including Elvis Presley, the Temptations, the Doors, the Rolling Stones, and Marvin Gaye—into America's living room. Sullivan died in 1974.

Today the theater is owned by a company that specializes in High Definition Television (HDTV) production. In 1990 and 1991, the stage was used to tape several concerts for the Music Television Network series "MTV Unplugged."

■ ELECTRIC LADY STUDIOS

52 West 8th Street, New York

In 1968, Jimi Hendrix and his manager Mike Jeffrey decided to open their own nightclub and paid $50,000 for a Greenwich Village building. The site had some precedence along that line—the Village Barn, a zany theme club decorated with milk pails, bales of hay, and country singers, had operated in the basement until the late Fifties, and a rock bar called the Generation Club had taken over in the mid-Sixties. But when Hendrix and Jeffrey discovered that they'd spent $300,000 that year on recording time at the Record Plant studio

The Ed Sullivan Theatre (New York City)

uptown, they decided to use the 8th Street site to build Hendrix a recording room of his own.

The construction dragged on for over a year and costs ultimately hit $1 million. Hendrix and his associates didn't learn until after the work began that Minetta Creek flows right under the basement floor, and the area was flooded for several months while a solution was sought. (Today, three different kinds of pumps keep the studios dry.) Hendrix also requisitioned special curving concrete walls to act as sound blocks—a subway line runs just a few feet from the building.

Finally, the unfinished cellar studio had its grand opening as Electric Lady. Hendrix attended the festivities, but had to leave early to catch a plane. Studio A is the only room in the complex he ever got to record in. He died less than a month after the opening.

The dream studio Jimi built reset the standard for the recording business. For the first time, great care (and considerable expense) had been devoted to creating comfort for musicians. For Electric Lady, designers commissioned psychedelic murals, built lounges, and installed dramatic lighting. The studio's first major client after Hendrix's death was Stevie Wonder, who worked throughout 1971 on tracks that would ultimately be used on his albums *Music of My Mind, Talking Book, Innervisions*, and *Fullfillingness First Finale*. Later, the Rolling Stones, Led Zeppelin, Aerosmith, and Kiss recorded at Electric Lady, and Patti Smith made *Horses* here in the summer of 1975.

■ THE FILLMORE EAST

105 Second Avenue, New York

One Greenwich Village generation knew the theater at 105 Second Avenue as Loewe's Commodore, a 1928 movie palace; for another, it was the Fillmore East, promoter Bill Graham's psychedelic showcase. A later generation came here when it was one of New York's more glorious gay discos, the Saint. Today's East Village denizens know it only as a boarded-up derelict.

The theater had a brief nascent life as a rock 'n' roll site before Graham took over—Vanilla Fudge, for example, made its New York debut here in July 1967. But the hall really started blooming on March 8, 1968, when it officially opened as the Fillmore East with a concert by Janis Joplin and Big Brother and the Holding Company.

Some other memorable Fillmore nights:

- Jimi Hendrix's Band of Gypsys performed here on the last night of the Sixties and the first night of the Seventies. Tickets were $5, $6, and $7. The group's only other public performance came a few weeks later at Madison Square Garden, where Jimi, suffering from bad LSD, apologized to the audience and stopped the concert early.
- The Jeff Beck Group played its first American concerts here in 1968, on a bill with the Grateful Dead. Beck's newly discovered lead singer, Rod Stewart, performed the first few songs hiding behind a bank of amplifiers. Observers believed he had a bad case of stage fright, but Stewart insisted in later years that he was suffering from throat trouble and was staying within reach of his stash of brandy.
- Led Zeppelin concluded its first American tour with a Fillmore concert on January 31, 1969. Iron Butterfly was scheduled to close the show, but refused to go on after Zeppelin's two hours of brain-roasting warmup.
- On June 6, 1971, John Lennon and Yoko Ono showed up to jam with Frank Zappa and the Mothers of Invention.
- The Allman Brothers Band played 140 concerts in 1971, and three of them—March 11 through 13—were at the Fillmore East. The shows were taped and became the band's landmark live album. Although the second set on March 13 didn't end until 4:40 A.M., the audience demanded and received an encore. The concert's last note was played at 7:05 A.M.—as daylight poured through the exit doors.

Graham was famous for his innovative pairings of bands. One bill, in April 1971, matched the Beach Boys with the Grateful Dead.

On June 27, 1971, just three years after the Fillmore opened, it closed with a concert by the J. Geils Band, the Allman Brothers Band, and Albert King.

■ THE GASLIGHT CAFE

116 MacDougal Street, New York

In the Fifties and Sixties, the Gaslight was the too-quintessential Village folk club, located in a basement. Through the night, Beat poets emoted and folk singers moaned.

In 1972, Bruce Springsteen auditioned for John Hammond, in the producer's CBS office. Hammond, who had agreed to listen to a few tunes, let Springsteen play for two hours, then arranged a showcase job for his new find at the Gaslight.

Today, the Gaslight is gone. The space has most recently been known as the Scrap Bar.

■ GERDE'S FOLK CITY

11 West 4th Street, New York

Gerde's, the Village folk haunt where Bob Dylan played his first New York club gigs in April 1961, is history. At its address now stands the Jewish Institute of Religion.

■ THE HARD ROCK CAFE

221 West 57th Street, New York

The New York Hard Rock features a guitar-shaped bar, leather outfits from the Ramones, Brian Jones' Vox Mark VI guitar, Prince's purple *Purple Rain* getup, and one of Elvis' Vegas-period stage jumpers. Now, as always, it's a popular stop for tourists.

Call for hours: 212-459-9320.

4 Pennsylvania Plaza, New York

Madison Square Garden events have run the gamut. The sublime: at a Thanksgiving show in 1974, John Lennon joined Elton John onstage for "Whatever Gets You Through the Night," "Lucy in the Sky with Diamonds," and "I Saw Her Standing There," in what was to be Lennon's last public performance. The ridiculous: Sly Stone married Kathy Silva onstage here in June 1974 (she filed for divorce in October).

In August 1971, the Concert for Bangladesh, starring George Harrison, Bob Dylan, Leon Russell, and Ringo Starr, was held at the Garden. Closing out the decade in September 1979, the Musicians United for Safe Energy (Jackson Browne, Bonnie Raitt, Bruce Springsteen, the Doobie Brothers, James Taylor, and Crosby, Stills, and Nash) performed here. The MUSE concerts were memorialized in a movie and a multi-disc album; both were titled *No Nukes*.

In fact, many Garden concerts have been memorialized on film and in song. The Rolling Stones' performances in November 1969 were recorded and released as *Get Yer Ya-Ya's Out!* and 1973 appearances by Led Zeppelin became the film *The Song Remains the Same.* Rick Nelson played an oldies show here in October 1971 and was hooted off the stage for not sticking to oldies. He later sang about the ordeal in "Garden Party," which went Top Ten in 1972.

Madison Square Garden also features pro basketball, hockey, and dog shows. Call 212-465-6741.

213 Park Avenue South, New York

Once one of New York's top restaurant/clubs, Max's Kansas City was frequented by the Andy Warhol crowd in the late Sixties; accordingly, the Velvet Underground had a brief residency. Other Max's residents include Aerosmith, who signed with Columbia after a stand here, and Debbie Harry, who worked in pre-Blondie days as a cocktail waitress.

It closed forever, long ago.

■ MEDIA SOUND

311 West 57th Street, New York

Originally a Baptist church, Media Sound boasted a cathedral ceiling and a staff of expert engineers—Mike DeLugg, Bob Clearmountain, and Tony Bongiovi all started here.

The studio kept busy by soliciting work from the world outside of rock 'n' roll, producing the prerecorded music for "The Ed Sullivan Show" and most of the early original music for "Sesame Street." On the rock side, T. Rex used the studio to record parts of its glitter monument—*Electric Warrior*.

The space has been extensively remodeled and is now a restaurant called Le Bar Bat. The phone number is 212-307-7228.

■ THE MERCER ARTS CENTER

Broadway Central Hotel, Broadway and 3rd Street, New York

The corner of Broadway and 3rd oozed history long before the New York Dolls discovered it. Actor John Wilkes Booth once played a theater that stood on the lot, and later the Broadway Central Hotel (which replaced the theater in the late nineteenth century) became a society gathering place and a clubhouse for the corrupt Tweed ring of city politicians. By the time the early Seventies rolled around, the place was tired and moth-eaten—perfect for an onslaught of punks with roaring guitars. A back section of the old hotel was remodeled into a complex of studios and theaters called the Mercer Arts Center, and quickly became home to the Dolls and other underground New Yorkers.

On August 3, 1973, part of the hotel collapsed, forcing demolition of the rest. An apartment building stands on the site now.

■ MTV'S FIRST STUDIO

Unitel Video, 515 West 57th Street, New York

The Music Television Network's first show was broadcast from Unitel's 57th Street studios on August 1, 1981. Since the programming couldn't be seen in New York City—Manhattan wasn't yet adequately wired for cable—the first-night party was held in Fort Lee, New Jersey.

Since then, MTV's moved to new studios on West 42nd Street.

■ THE MUSEUM OF TELEVISION AND RADIO

25 West 52nd Street, New York

Thousands of hours of great programming (including lots of rock 'n' roll: the "Ed Sullivan" appearances of Elvis and the Beatles are the most-requested tapes) are kept in the Museum of Television and Radio in its state-of-the-art computerized library.

The suggested entrance donation is $5; call 212-621-6715 for hours and more information.

■ NBC-TV STUDIO 8H

30 Rockefeller Plaza, New York

"Saturday Night Live" has been taped from NBC's large soundstage in Rockefeller Plaza since 1975. In addition to all the great comedy, the show was responsible for some of rock's finest television, including John Belushi's duet with Joe Cocker, Devo's national debut, the Rolling Stones' ragged *Some Girls* set, and top-notch performances by The Band, the B-52s, the Blues Brothers, David Bowie, Jackson Browne, Ray Charles, Elvis Costello, the Grateful Dead, Billy Joel, Bette Midler, Van Morrison, Randy Newman, Nirvana, Tom Petty and the Heartbreakers, Prince, Public Enemy, Bonnie Raitt, Paul Simon, Patti Smith, Talking Heads, James Taylor, Loudon Wainwright III, Tom Waits, and Frank Zappa.

The show is a tough ticket, but NBC tours usually offer visitors a peek at the studio from a balcony window. Call 212-664-4444.

■ THE PEPPERMINT LOUNGE

128 West 45th Street, New York

A famous nightclub, the Peppermint Lounge was also Home of the Twist. A tall new building now stands at its address.

■ THE POWER STATION

441 West 53rd Street, New York

T he Power Station recording studio started up in 1977, when Bob Walters, a big-band musician and bandleader, and Tony Bongiovi (who'd talked his way into an engineering job at Motown as a teenager) split from Media Sound.

Operating out of a former Con Edison utility plant on the West Side (some of the concrete floors are three feet thick), the Power Station has a reputation for great "live"-sounding rooms. The studio recorded and mixed Chic's influential disco hits here, as well as albums by Ian Hunter, Foghat, and the Kinks. Bruce Springsteen recorded *The River* at the Power Station in 1979 and 1980, and held sessions for *Born in the USA* in the early Eighties.

■ PYTHIAN TEMPLE STUDIOS

135 West 70th Street, New York

W hen 135 West 70th Street was the meeting hall for the Knights of Pythias, Decca used the building's ballroom as a recording studio. "Rock Around the Clock"—a little number by Bill Haley and the Comets that would go on to sell more than 22 million copies—was recorded here in April 1954.

The building still looks like a weird temple, but now it's a condominium.

1260 Avenue of the Americas, New York

Radio City opened as a posh Art Deco movie palace in December 1932; now it's known for good concerts (and, of course, the Rockettes). James Taylor played here November 3, 1972, the night he married Carly Simon.

For a time, Radio City also had its own downstairs recording studio, and in February 1976 the Ramones used the space (it was known as Plaza Sound) to record their debut album. Total recording time was one week, total cost was $6,400. The band got a bargain because there were no freight elevators to the place and they had to lug all their equipment up and down the stairs.

■ RCA STUDIOS

55 East 24th and 110 West 44th Streets, New York

RCA Victor's recording headquarters were on East 24th Street until the summer of 1969, when the company built state-of-the-art facilities farther uptown. Elvis Presley cut "Hound Dog," "Don't Be Cruel," and "Blue Suede Shoes" in 24th Street's Studio A in 1956.

The 24th Street building now houses classrooms and offices for Baruch College, but the 44th Street plant became BMG Studios in the late Eighties and remains a popular place for soundtracks and other types of recordings.

■ THE RECORD PLANT

321 West 44th Street, New York

Hendrix, Aerosmith, and Kiss define the Record Plant sound—it was the all-time hard-rock studio. The Jimi Hendrix Experience recorded *Electric Ladyland* here in 1968, often drafting musicians from the nearby Scene club to come to the studio and jam; one such session, featuring Steve Winwood on organ and Jack Casady on bass, became "Voodoo Chile." Bruce Springsteen recorded most of *Born to Run* at the Plant in spring 1975, and returned for *Darkness on the Edge of Town* in spring 1978.

John Lennon was going home from a mixing session here on the night he was murdered.

The Record Plant closed in the late Eighties. Most recently, the ground-floor space where the two main studios were has been occupied by nightclubs. Upper-floor recording and mixing rooms are operated under the name 3-2-1 Studio.

■ **THE SCENE**

301 West 46th Street, New York

The Scene, a cave-like dive, was a favorite after-hours jam spot for Jimi Hendrix (especially while he was recording *Electric Ladyland* at the Record Plant), Eric Clapton, Led Zeppelin, the Doors, and others. There were nights when Janis Joplin, Jimi Hendrix, and Jim Morrison were all in the room at the same time.

A fellow named Steve Paul ran the club, so it was often referred to as Steve Paul's Scene. But the Scene split a long time ago.

■ **SHEA STADIUM**

126th Street and Roosevelt Avenue, Queens

The Beatles' 1965 show at Shea Stadium set the world pop-concert record at 55,600 (even Mick Jagger and Keith Richards were in the audience). In 1966 the Beatles played the home of the Mets again, to an equally large and shrieking crowd.

■ **THE SILVER FACTORY**

231 East 47th Street

Pop artist Andy Warhol lived in the Silver Factory (so-named for its silver-paint-and-aluminum-foil-decor statement) from 1963 to 1968. While here, Warhol became friendly with the Velvet Underground and even designed their first album cover featuring a peel-off banana. The Rolling Stones' *Sticky Fingers* and *Love You Live* covers are other Warhol creations, as is the band's famous lapping-tongue logo.

The building was demolished soon after Warhol moved out.

Beatlemania at Shea Stadium—August 15, 1965

■ STRAWBERRY FIELDS

Central Park at 72nd Street, New York

Strawberry Fields is a small area of Central Park set aside in tribute to John Lennon. It's located just across the street from the Dakota, Lennon's home at the time of his death. The centerpiece of Strawberry Fields is a flat stone monument, set into a path near the park entrance, which carries the word "Imagine."

■ STUDIO 54

254 West 54th Street, New York

Studio 54 was the daddy of all discos, famous for jet-set high jinks (Mick and Bianca were regulars). But when disco died, 54 did, too. Now it's the Ritz, one of Manhattan's better concert halls. The phone number is 212-541-8900.

■ THE VILLAGE GATE

160 Bleecker Street, New York

One of the major New York nightclubs, the Village Gate began in a basement and eventually expanded to three levels. It's famous for jazz, but certain pop lore has grown around it. For example, one source lists it as the site of Aretha Franklin's New York debut. According to another story, the first psychedelic light show in New York took place here during a 1966 Byrds concert.

The Gate still swings. Call 212-475-5120.

Saugerties

■ BIG PINK

2188 Stoll Road, West Saugerties

A no-frills house, Big Pink was home base for Bob Dylan and The Band in the summer and fall of 1967, and also served as a crude recording studio. The albums resulting from sessions here were classics: The Band's *Music From Big Pink* and Dylan's *The Basement Tapes* (released years after the original tapes had made bootleg history). At the time of the recordings, Dylan was in seclusion following his 1966 motorcycle crash. It's estimated that he and The Band committed more than 150 songs to tape between June and October of 1967.

The house has been altered since then, but it's still painted pink and it also continues to attract music-business people. It is now owned by a bass player who lives in New York City; the house's tenants have included a guitar maker and a trader in rare classical music albums.

Watkins Glen

■ WATKINS GLEN RACEWAY

Route 16 and Meade's Hill Road, near Watkins Glen

The Watkins Glen raceway was the site of the largest rock festival ever. About 600,000 people attended the huge Summer Jam concert in July 1973, and the headliners were the Allman Brothers Band, the Grateful Dead, and The Band.

The raceway is located south of the town of Watkins Glen, off Highway 414. (The big races are held in the summer.)

Westbury

■ D'ANDREA MANUFACTURING COMPANY

900 Shames Drive, Westbury, Long Island

D'Andrea, the world's largest manufacturer of guitar picks, was founded in 1922 in Manhattan by Luigi D'Andrea; his grandson, Tony, runs the factory (relocated to Long Island) today. Picks of all shapes, colors, and materials (including celluloid, nylon, and something called Delrin) are manufactured here, and at least one new model is introduced every year. To date, the company has created 10,000 different pick designs.

D'Andrea has also done custom work for many top guitarists, including Les Paul, Eddie Van Halen, Aerosmith, Bon Jovi, Judas Priest, the Ramones, the Beatles, Skid Row, and ZZ Top.

Woodstock

■ BOB DYLAN CRASH SITE

Zena Road, south of Highway 212, Woodstock

Bob Dylan was tooling along on his Triumph 500 motorcycle on July 29, 1966, when the back wheel locked and tossed him over the handlebars. He was disabled for eighteen months following the wreck.

There is some controversy about this event, including theories that the accident never happened and that Dylan had other reasons to hide for a year and a half. But according to a local lawman who was on the scene, the accident was real, and it happened one mile south of Highway 212 where Zena Road takes a sharp turn, near a rustic barn sometimes called the Old Zena Mill.

PENNSYLVANIA

Nazareth

■ MARTIN GUITAR COMPANY

---

510 Sycamore Street, Nazareth

Perhaps the best-known maker of acoustic guitars in the world, Martin has been in business in Nazareth since 1833. The original factory, at 10 West North Street, is now a guitar makers' supply shop. The company's current manufacturing plant was built in 1964 and expanded in 1972, and the new buildings also house a fine little museum.

A free tour of the plant is conducted every day at 1:15 P.M. (promptly), and there's a shop that sells memorabilia and guitar accessories. Nazareth is just north of Bethlehem. Call 800-633-2060 for more information.

Philadelphia

■ JFK STADIUM

Broad Street, near Pattison Avenue, Philadelphia

Live Aid, the brainchild of Boomtown Rat Bob Geldof, was two simultaneous concerts in London and Philadelphia, designed to raise funds to feed the world's hungry. The shows (held on July 13, 1985) were televised live by MTV, which understandably exploited every opportunity for self-promotion. Live Aid was, nonetheless, one of the decade's musical highlights. Performers at the Philadelphia show included Crosby, Stills, and Nash, Bob Dylan, Led Zeppelin, Joan Baez, Mick Jagger, Neil Young, Tina Turner, and Teddy Pendergrass.

JFK Stadium was built in the Twenties, and torn down in the Nineties. A new indoor arena, the Spectrum II, will be built on its lot.

OPPOSITE: *Live Aid crowd—July 13, 1985 (Philadelphia)* © Ken Regan/Camera 5

■ SIGMA SOUND STUDIOS

212 North 12th Street, Philadelphia

When engineer Joe Tarsia took over Sigma in 1968, the studio had already produced many hits, including records by Bobby Rydell and the Dovells. But Tarsia, working with producers Kenny Gamble and Leon Huff, took Sigma in a new direction—and ultimately into a new dimension. The team gave birth to the distinctive sound of Philadelphia Soul, by far the best music on AM radio in the early Seventies.

The studio created dozens of hits in those years. Later it segued into disco with groups such as the Salsoul Orchestra and the Trammps, but Sigma continued to draw pilgrims from other branches of rock who were enchanted with Philly Soul. Robert Palmer came here to cut *Double Fun;* David Bowie did *Young Americans;* Todd Rundgren recorded "Hello It's Me."

■ SIGMA SOUND RECORDINGS

The Delfonics	"La La Means I Love You"
	"Didn't I Blow Your Mind This Time"
The Stylistics	"You Are Everything"
	"Betcha by Golly Wow"
	"Stone in Love With You"
	"You Make Me Feel Brand New"
	"Rock and Roll Baby"
O'Jays	"Backstabbers"
	"Love Train"
	"For the Love of Money"
	"I Love Music"
Harold Melvin and the Blue Notes	"Bad Luck"
	"If You Don't Know Me by Now"
	"The Love I Lost"
	"Wake Up Everybody"

Billy Paul	"Me and Mrs. Jones"
Joe Simon	"Drowning in a Sea of Love"
The Spinners	"I'll Be Around" "Could It Be I'm Falling in Love" "One of a Kind Love Affair" "Then Came You" (with Dionne Warwick) "Rubberband Man"
The Three Degrees	"When Will I See You Again"
MFSB	"TSOP"
The Jacksons	"Enjoy Yourself"

■ WALK OF FAME

South Broad Street, Philadelphia

The Philadelphia Music Alliance (which also sponsors music-in-the-schools programs) oversees its own Walk of Fame, which starts in front of the Philadelphia Academy of Music and runs to the University of the Arts. All styles of music are represented on the pavement; pop and rock honorees include Frankie Avalon, Dick Clark, Jim Croce, Bill Haley, Patti LaBelle, Harold Melvin and the Blue Notes, Teddy Pendergrass, Todd Rundgren, Bobby Rydell, Bessie Smith, and Grover Washington, Jr.

Farther south on Broad Street is South Philadelphia High, which has been a veritable music-talent farm (most successfully harvested by Dick Clark). Mario Lanza, Frankie Avalon, Chubby Checker, and Eddie Fisher are a few famous alumni.

46th and Market Streets, Philadelphia

In October 1952, WFIL, a local television station, began programming an experimental afternoon show, calling it "Bandstand." Bob Horn and Lee Stewart were the hosts, and people tuned in to see local kids dancing to the latest pop songs. Visiting stars promoted their current hits by lip-synching along to the records, and there was also a rate-a-record segment. The format for "American Bandstand" was set from the start, even before it was called "American Bandstand."

At the time, Dick Clark was an announcer and disc jockey for WFIL's radio side and sometimes played substitute host for "Bandstand." Stewart left the show after a few years; then, in the summer of 1956, Horn had a meltdown—there were drunk-driving arrests (WFIL's owner, the *Philadelphia Inquirer*, was running a splashy anti-drunk-driving campaign at the time), allegations of sexual improprieties with young fans, and tax trouble. Clark was asked to take over. He was 24, and he never looked back. The next year, ABC picked up the show and ran it nationwide.

The show's air time (2:45 P.M.) was dictated by the class schedule at nearby West Catholic High, which dismissed its students at 2:30. The studio held 150 dancers, who were aged fourteen to seventeen—no older, no younger. Until 1957, when Clark decided to integrate the show, all the dancers were white. One day in 1960 he noticed a black couple doing the Twist on the show. Immediately, he had a local kid named Ernest Evans (Chubby Checker to you) re-record Hank Ballard's original cut of the song and began playing the new version regularly on "Bandstand."

The show and its stars became immensely popular. A riot broke out on 46th Street the day Fabian and Frankie Avalon showed up at the studio together—mounted police had to be called out to disperse the crowd of 1,000 hysterical girls. Even the "Bandstand" regulars—a group of about thirty kids called the Committee—were celebrities and got thousands of fan letters.

Clark had a finger in every piece of the musical pie—talent management, music publishing, record pressing, label making, distribution, domestic and foreign rights, motion pictures, and merchandising. Each week, he and producer Tony Mammarella picked the Top Ten themselves. Teen dreams Fabian, Bobby Rydell, James Darren, Connie Francis, Bobby Darin, and Frankie

Dick Clark at WFIL Studios, the Philadelphia home of "American Bandstand"

Avalon were all essentially Dick Clark creations, images manufactured for national saturation on "Bandstand." A favorite hangout for Clark and his crew was the Brown Jug (an Irish saloon near the studio) and in a back room there, Clark received recording-industry hustlers—label reps and an assortment of promo men.

Clark divested himself of most of his music-related business interests (worth millions of dollars) before the payola scandals hit in 1959. Still, he was a major subject of the Senate investigation into payola—the practice of kickbacks and bribes that was rampant in the music industry. At the time, Pop Singer's drugstore at Market and Farragut streets was a gathering place for the show's dancers, and Clark, fearing that his work phone was bugged by the authorities, would only confer with his lawyers on the pay phone at Pop's.

While other careers toppled around him (notably Alan Freed's and Mammarella's), Clark stood his ground and ultimately emerged relatively unscathed. One point of contention between Clark and Congress during the payola investigation centered on instrumentalist Duane Eddy. Clark owned a piece of Eddy's publishing business, and could potentially profit from sales of Eddy's records. And Clark had been playing an *awful lot* of Eddy's records on "Bandstand." But Clark had a ready answer: the show's format called for an instrumental tune to be played before every half-hour break, and Eddy was, of course, king of the instrumentalists.

Clark moved "Bandstand" to California in March 1964; while there he launched "Where the Action Is," an afternoon show that sometimes taped on the beach in Malibu. That's a long way from 46th Street.

Today, WFIL's old building is hauntingly empty, used by Philadelphia's Public Broadcasting Service affiliate as a warehouse. The main studio holds old flats and boxes, and the only sign that the structure has anything to do with airwaves are the satellite dishes in the fenced parking lot. Touring the building is not possible. There's nothing left to see anyway.

Sharon Hill

■ BESSIE SMITH'S GRAVE

Mount Lawn Cemetery, 84th Street and Hook Road, Sharon Hill

The grave of blues pioneer Bessie Smith remained unmarked from her death in 1937 until August 1970, when Janis Joplin and Juanita Green (a Philadelphia woman who had worked for Smith) bought and set up a tombstone there. At the time, Joplin herself had only two months to live.

Not far from Smith's monument is the grave of Tammi Terrell, Marvin Gaye's brilliant mid-Sixties duet partner. She collapsed onstage while performing with Gaye in 1967; the brain tumor that caused the seizure killed her three years later. Terrell is buried under her real name—Thomasina Montgomery.

Mount Lawn is a small graveyard near the Philadelphia airport; the phone number is 215-586-8220.

York

■ HARLEY-DAVIDSON PLANT AND MUSEUM

1425 Eden Road, east of York

The hour-and-a-half plant tour (they provide you with safety glasses!) and antique–Harley-Davidson museum are free, and there's also a nice gift shop. About 35,000 people visit every year.

Drive east on Route 30 out of York, then take a left at the third light after Interstate 83. Call 717-848-1177 to check on the tour schedule.

RHODE ISLAND

Newport

■ FREEBODY PARK

Freebody Street, near Memorial Boulevard

Bob Dylan was the hit of the Newport Folk Festival at Freebody Park in 1963—he even led an audience singalong on "Blowin' in the Wind." But his 1965 set was another story. Dylan had returned to the festival backed by the Paul Butterfield Blues Band and the loud, electric program they played enraged the assembled folkies, who hooted the band off the stage. Dylan returned a little later to do an acoustic number, but the shift had hit the fan: Woody Guthrie's heir had become a rocker.

Aside from some 1991 landscaping, the park is little changed from its folk-festival days. From Belleview Avenue, go east on Memorial Boulevard for about a block. Look for the Tennis Hall of Fame—it's just west of the park.

Providence

■ THE RHODE ISLAND SCHOOL OF DESIGN

Benefit Street, Providence

Talking Heads David Byrne, Chris Frantz, and Tina Weymouth met at the Rhode Island School of Design as students in the early Seventies.

Benefit Street, a main route into and out of town, cuts right through campus.

VIRGINIA

Norfolk

■ LEGRAND RECORDS

Princess Anne and Colonial Avenues, Norfolk

Legrand Records only had a few hits, but they were whoppers. First, in 1959, Legrand owner Frank Guida released more than two dozen different regional versions of "High School U.S.A."—a daffy novelty tune that shouted a list of high school names. The next year, inspired by a sign in a nearby deli window (a leftover from World War II that said Buy U.S. Bonds), Guida gave Gary U.S. Bonds his name. Bonds recorded "New Orleans" and "Quarter to Three" at Legrand—classic productions that influenced Phil Spector, the Beatles, Bruce Springsteen, and almost everybody else. Both songs were recorded in this little studio. In 1963, Jimmy Soul had a number-one hit for Guida—"If You Wanna Be Happy."

Frank Guida is still at it, watching over his publishing mini-empire and promoting his role in creating the "Norfolk Sound." The original Legrand building has been torn down; today, Arthur's Drugstore stands where Bonds and saxophonist Gene "Daddy G" Barge once wailed.

WASHINGTON, D.C.

■ THE CAPITOL MALL

In the spring of 1983, Interior Secretary James Watt banned the Beach Boys from playing in the annual Fourth of July celebration held on the Capitol Mall—they attracted "the wrong element," he said—and proceeded to book Wayne Newton for the date. However, the Boys of the Endless Summer were vindicated when they received a personal invitation from the Reagans (who were, to their credit, big Beach Boys fans) to play a mid-June benefit concert for the Special Olympics.

■ THE HARD ROCK CAFE

999 E Street NW, Washington, D.C.

Beatles memorabilia dominates the collection at the Washington Hard Rock—most notably the piccolo trumpet heard in "Penny Lane" and "All You Need Is Love." A National Glenwood Series 98 guitar once favored by Bob Dylan is also on display.

Call 202-737-7625 for more information.

■ LISNER AUDITORIUM

730 21st Street NW, Washington, D.C.

In 1977, Lisner Auditorium was the recording site for Little Feat's live album, *Waiting for Columbus*. The group's founder, Lowell George, was a great slide-guitar player and singer, described by a friend as the offspring of Orson Wells and Howlin' Wolf. He returned to the Lisner on June 28, 1979, during a tour to promote his first solo album. The next day, at age 34, he died of a heart attack.

The theater is located on the George Washington University campus. Call 202-994-1500 for ticket information.

■ THE U.S. CAPITOL

The Mall, Washington, D.C.

The Special Subcommittee on Legislative Oversight of the Committee on Interstate and Foreign Commerce, chaired by Representative Oren Harris, met in late 1959 and early 1960 to get to the bottom of payola in the music business (which, many older folks were certain, was the only reason for rock 'n' roll's popularity). As mentioned earlier, Dick Clark and Alan Freed were the star witnesses. Clark fared better than Freed, who was hounded from the business and beset soon after by tax and health troubles; he died in his early forties, a broken man.

In 1985, the Senate Commerce Committee held hearings here on the negative effects of rock 'n' roll lyrics. Leading the charge against rock "pornography" were Tipper Gore, Susan Baker, Georgie Packwood, and Nancy Thurmond—all wives of prominent government movers and shakers. Frank Zappa, John Denver, and Dee Snider were witnesses for the First Amendment.

Call 202-224-3121 for tour information.

THE SOUTH

ALABAMA

Huntsville

■ OAKWOOD COLLEGE

Huntsville

L ittle Richard Penniman was at the top of the rock 'n' roll heap in 1957, selling millions of records, making movies, performing internationally. But during a tour of Australia, he heard of the *Sputnik* launch and experienced a religious rebirth. He renounced rock 'n' roll and threw his expensive jewelry into Sydney Harbor.

Penniman returned to the United States and enrolled at Oakwood College, a Seventh-Day Adventist school founded in 1896. Although he occasionally lapsed back into the secular realm—appearing on television talk shows and acting—Little Richard never regained the momentum of '57.

The college is northwest of downtown Huntsville. Call 205-726-7000 for directions.

Montgomery

■ OAKWOOD CEMETERY ANNEX

1304 Upper Wetumpka Road, Montgomery

H ank Williams, symbol of rock's country roots, was found dead in his car on New Year's Day, 1953. He's buried in the annex of Oakwood Cemetery. The cemetery is near downtown Montgomery. To find Williams' marker, bear right once inside the entrance. Hours are 7 A.M. to 3:30 P.M., and the phone number is 205-240-4630.

Muscle Shoals

■ THE ALABAMA MUSIC HALL OF FAME

Highway 72, Tuscumbia

Opened in 1990, the Alabama Music Hall of Fame celebrates the state's many contributions to popular music, including Alabama (the group), Nat "King" Cole, Eddie Floyd, Donna Godchaux, Vern Gosdin, W. C. Handy, Emmylou Harris, Eddie Kendrick, Jim Nabors, Sam Phillips, Martha Reeves, Lionel Richie, Ray Sawyer, Tommy Shaw, Percy Sledge, Sun Ra, Toni Tenille, Willie Mae "Big Mama" Thornton, Joe Tex, Hank Williams, and Wet Willie.

Country music dominates the display—for example, the band Alabama has donated its touring bus and the vehicle's now parked in the middle of the hall—but the museum recognizes performers from all musical camps. Some rock 'n' roll highlights:

- The embroidered hippie dress worn by Donna Godchaux, one-time Grateful Dead vocalist, at the band's storied concerts near the Great Pyramids of Egypt.
- The contract signed by Sun recording studio owner Sam Phillips that gave over Elvis Presley to RCA. Phillips is a native of the Muscle Shoals area.
- The suit Lionel Richie wore during the taping of "We Are the World."
- Prominently displayed, Jim Nabors' Marine Corps uniform from "Gomer Pyle, U.S.M.C."
- An eye patch and beat-up hat belonging to Dr. Hook and the Medicine Show's front man, Ray Sawyer.
- A placard telling the story of Sam Lay, a Birmingham native who went on to semi-fame as a drummer for Chess Records in Chicago and, later, as Bob Dylan's drummer on "Like a Rolling Stone."

One corner of the museum space is devoted to telling the story of the Muscle Shoals sound and features a multi-episode video presentation. Be mindful that Muscle Shoals history can be vexing to the uninitiated. A lot of sublime music has come out of this stretch of the Tennessee River, but so has much political feuding.

Wise pilgrims will stop at the museum first for a complete audio-video briefing on all the local doings. And while you're there, take a moment to get a deeper feel for the place. The museum backs right up to a real cotton field, and visitors from outside the South, especially, should have a good long look at it. To really understand this part of the world, you've got to understand cotton.

Call 800-239-2643 for hours and information. Admission is about $6, parking is free, and there's a gift shop on the premises.

■ **FAME STUDIOS**

603 East Avalon Avenue, Muscle Shoals

Rick Hall, owner of Fame Studios, is the patriarch of the modern recording era in the Shoals. Most of the musicians and engineers credited with creating the funky Muscle Shoals sound got their start with Hall and like most great men, he's been called stubborn, and he's gathered and discarded collaborators along the way.

Hall has operated studios out of several locations. The first, Florence Alabama Music Enterprises (spelled F.A.M.E.), was located above a drug store in Florence; the next leased space in a tobacco warehouse. Later, Hall made the move to 603 Avalon.

The big time found Fame in early 1966, when Atlantic Records producer Jerry Wexler brought Wilson Pickett down from Memphis. Wexler had already done business in the Shoals area, purchasing the distribution rights for Percy Sledge's epochal "When a Man Loves a Woman," which Sledge had recorded in Quinn Ivy's small studio in nearby Sheffield. In 1966, Wexler, Pickett, Hall, and Fame's house band recorded "Land of 1,000 Dances," "Mustang Sally," and "Funky Broadway." The discography could stop there and Fame would still qualify as hallowed ground.

But then Wexler followed *that* success by bringing Aretha Franklin to town in January 1967. At Fame, she recorded "I Never Loved a Man (the Way I Love You)" and preliminary tracks for "Do Right Woman (Do Right Man)." But the sessions ended abruptly after an in-studio blowup between Franklin, her husband, and the local backing musicians. Aretha left town and Wexler followed, severing his relationship with Hall. Later, some of the Muscle Shoals musicians were summoned to Atlantic's New York studios to help finish Franklin's first album. "Respect" was one of the results of those sessions.

But Fame's hit-making years were far from over. James and Bobby Purify recorded "I'm Your Puppet" here, Joe Tex followed with "Hold What You've Got," Clarence Carter made "Slip Away" and "Patches," and Wilson Pickett recorded his own version of "Hey Jude" (backed by Duane Allman on guitar). Hall even made chart successes of the Osmond Brothers ("One Bad Apple"), Mac Davis ("Baby Don't Get Hooked on Me"), and Paul Anka ("Having My Baby").

The Muscle Shoals area is not just some dusty little dot on the map of northwest Alabama—it's *several* dusty little dots, representing the neighboring towns of Florence, Muscle Shoals, Sheffield, and Tuscumbia. That there are towns here at all is due to the river, the big hydroelectric dam on it, and industry. In addition to funky music, textiles and aluminum are the specialties of the Shoals.

Much of the area's studio production—including most of Fame's work—has turned to country music. In that field, Hall's helped make hits for Jerry Reed, T. G. Sheppard, and Shenandoah. He's still a busy man, and sessions continue in his studios daily. Fame sits approximately in the middle of the cluster of towns, near the intersection of Avalon and Woodward. The building carries a sign that says "Where It All Started."

■ MUSCLE SHOALS SOUND STUDIO I

3614 Jackson Highway, Sheffield

There's a paradox about Muscle Shoals: most of the musicians who created the Muscle Shoals sound—a subtle, funky, soulful blend of styles—are white. That fact often comes as a surprise to people who know the sound only from records.

One explanation is geographic: the players were exposed in early life to the music beamed into northern Alabama via radio from New Orleans, Jackson, Memphis, Nashville, and the Mississippi Delta. They had the entire spectrum of Southern soul, blues, country, rockabilly, and more at their fingertips. Another more fanciful theory is geologic. This theory, which is actually men-

The Allman Brothers at the original Muscle Shoals Sound Studio (Muscle Shoals, Alabama)

tioned in the literature, holds that the mountains in the area (large hills, really) allow a special quality of bass sound to be captured in the recording process.

The best-known purveyors of the Muscle Shoals sound came together at Fame Studios in 1964, but left Fame in 1969 to launch their own studio. The musicians—guitarist Jimmy Johnson, drummer Roger Hawkins, pianist Berry Beckett, and bassist David Hood—moved into an old coffin factory on Jackson Highway in Sheffield.

With some backing from Atlantic Records, the liberated session men went to work. The first big hit to come out of the factory was R. B. Greaves' "Take a Letter, Maria." Soon after, Cher cut an album here and called it *3614 Jackson Highway*. And the Rolling Stones came through en route to Altamont, stayed three days to work on *Sticky Fingers,* and recorded perhaps their greatest single, "Brown Sugar." They also cut "Wild Horses" and "You Got to Move," with Jimmy Johnson at the mixing console. The Stones filmed the "Wild Horses" playback scene featured about midway through *Gimme Shelter* in the control room here; Keith Richards claims he and Mick Jagger wrote the chorus to the song in the studio's bathroom.

Later, Paul Simon came to town to record one track for *There Goes Rhymin' Simon* and ended up staying for several, including the hit "Kodachrome." (Simon later returned with Art Garfunkel to make "My Little Town.") Bob Seger cut much of his Seventies material here—including tracks for *Night Moves* and *Stranger in Town* and the singles "Katmandu," "Old Time Rock 'n' Roll," and "We've Got Tonight." Rod Stewart's *Atlantic Crossing* and the single "Tonight's the Night," and most of the Staples Singers' greatest hits, including "I'll Take You There," were recorded here, too.

The Jackson Highway studio closed when the team left in 1978 for a larger space, but the old stone-faced building still stands. Jackson Highway is a meandering diagonal road that juts off to the southwest from Highway 43. The studio's clearly marked shell is on the east side of the road, opposite a cemetery.

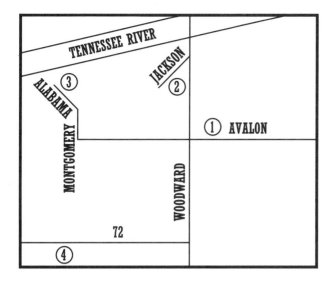

The Muscle Shoals area:
1) *Fame Studios*
2) *The Jackson Highway studio*
3) *Muscle Shoals Sound Studios*
4) *The Alabama Music Hall of Fame*

■ **MUSCLE SHOALS SOUND STUDIO II**

1000 Alabama Avenue, Sheffield

Muscle Shoals Sound Studio's founders (who were also known as the Muscle Shoals Rhythm Section or, as Lynyrd Skynyrd dubbed them in "Sweet Home Alabama," the Swampers) moved to this large bunker at 1000 Alabama Avenue in 1978. Constructed at the turn of the century as a power plant for the town of Sheffield, the building was later converted into a Naval Reserve Center. Now the complex holds a few studios, offices for the players, and an uncanny collection of gold records.

The Swampers' first major project at the new location was Bob Dylan's *Slow Train Coming*. Since then, they've worked on Dire Straits' *Communique*, Delbert McClinton's "Giving It Up for Your Love," Bob Seger's *Against the Wind*, and Glenn Frey's *No Fun Aloud*. Lately the studio has been making country hits for the Oak Ridge Boys, T. Graham Brown, the Forester Sisters, and John Conlee.

Drive through Muscle Shoals and Sheffield on either 2nd Street or Avalon. Turn north on Montgomery, then northwest on the diagonal Alabama Avenue. The studio is in a beautiful location—surrounded by trees, right on the banks of the Tennessee River. Informal and limited studio tours are sometimes conducted before 10:30 A.M. Call 205-381-2060.

2nd Street, Sheffield

In the Sixties, Quinn Ivy, local record store owner and producer, operated Quinvy Studios out of a single-story building with one large room. (It had probably been a restaurant.) Ivy brought singer Percy Sledge and some Muscle Shoals musicians together in his little studio at Christmas in 1965 and the result was "When a Man Loves a Woman" (which Sledge had recently created during an improvised love lament in a Sheffield club). In the studio, Ivy, Sledge, and the players (including some members of the Muscle Shoals Rhythm Section) took a few passes at the tune over a period of days, but an early take was the one eventually released, complete with an overdub of charming, out-of-tune horns.

Quinvy Studios was in the second building east of Montgomery on the south side of 2nd Street—now an empty lot. Quinn Ivy teaches accounting at a local university.

ARKANSAS

Helena

■ THE DELTA CULTURAL CENTER

95 Missouri Street, Helena

If you want to get to the root of Delta blues, the Delta Cultural Center, a superb little museum built into Helena's old railroad station, is a perfect place to start. The displays set the scene for an informed exploration of Delta life, and an atmospheric corner exhibit covers all the pertinent Arkansas musicians, including Levon Helm, Conway Twitty, Al Green, and many of the blues greats.

The streets in Helena *crawl* with blues history. In the Thirties and Forties, Helena and West Helena were major destinations for all the Delta blues men. Robert Johnson, Sonny Boy Williamson (the second one), Honeyboy Edwards, Howlin' Wolf, and dozens of other legends played street corners in town by day and then moved to outlying juke joints after dark. Today, Helena is no longer the little Chicago it once was, but it is ideally located for day trips to other Delta blues landmarks, including Clarksdale (home to the Delta Blues Museum, Stackhouse Records, and the notorious crossroads of highways 49 and 61—the "Crossroads" of the Robert Johnson and Cream fame), the Robert Johnson Memorial near Morgan City, Dockery Farms, Sonny Boy II's grave in somewhat-nearby Tutwiler, and the official Southern and Dog railroad crossing in Moorhead. The annual King Biscuit Blues Festival is held on Cherry Street during the second week of October.

Helena is right on the Mississippi, about an hour south of Memphis. Just take Highway 61, turn west onto Highway 49, and cross the river.

■ **KFFA RADIO**

Highway 185, outside Helena

Helena is home to KFFA radio's daily burst of living history, the "King Biscuit Time" blues music program. The program started in 1941 and has run somewhat continuously since (it took a short break during the early Eighties), airing from a number of locations around town. The syndicated radio rock-concert show of the Seventies borrowed its name from this original King Biscuit.

Back when the show started, the blues was played live on the air. Rice Miller (who took the name Sonny Boy Williamson when the first Sonny Boy was stabbed to death in Chicago) was one of the early on-air stars, along with Robert Jr. Lockwood and others. Sonny Payne, a "King Biscuit" announcer in the old days, runs the show now, playing records and announcing ads for flour and cornmeal every weekday afternoon from 12:15 to 12:45.

The station's actual trailer-housed studios are outside of town, next to a field with an old Sonny Boy Corn Meal truck parked in it. Call 501-338-8361 for schedules and information on seeing the "King Biscuit" show live.

FLORIDA

Gainesville

■ DUB'S

4560 NW 13th Street, Gainesville

Tom Petty grew up in Gainesville, a college town (the University of Florida) in north-central Florida. According to Gainesville legend, young Tom once traded his slingshot for a stack of his buddy's Elvis Presley records. Later, he traveled with an uncle to visit the set of *Follow That Dream,* a Presley movie filming nearby. Petty saw Elvis in action that day and decided to make rock 'n' roll his life's work.

In the years between Petty's first Elvis sighting and worldwide stardom, he played just about every bar, club, and fraternity house in town, starting with his first date at fourteen in a local Moose lodge. At Dub's, Petty's band Mudcrutch, which included future Heartbreakers Mike Campbell and Benmont Tench, played backup music for topless dancers.

Dub's is closed now, but the building still stands on 13th Street, which is what State Highway 441 (mentioned in Petty's "American Girl") becomes on its way through Gainesville.

Golden Beach

■ 461 OCEAN BOULEVARD

461 Ocean Boulevard, Golden Beach

In the late Sixties, Criteria Studios founder Mack Emerman arranged to use the little house at 461 Ocean Boulevard as a base for musicians recording at the studios. Eric Clapton lived here while recording his follow-up to *Layla* in 1974, and eventually named the album after his temporary address. Clapton also posed for the jacket photo standing in the house's beach-front backyard.

Visitors who want to recreate the photo must approach the house from beach-side. The swooping palm on the album jacket died years ago, and a swimming pool has been added to the backyard, so the view has changed considerably since it was photographed for *461 Ocean Boulevard*. Ocean Boulevard is also called Highway A1A (and, in Miami Beach, Collins Avenue). There is no street parking near the house, and the nearest parking area, a block south, is off-limits. The beach is private property from the high-water mark to the yard—cross that line and you're a trespasser.

Jacksonville

■ ROBERT E. LEE HIGH SCHOOL

1200 South McDuff Avenue, Jacksonville

The founding members of Lynyrd Skynyrd were students at Robert E. Lee High in the early Seventies, struggling to find a balance between schoolwork and extracurricular activities. As members of the Jacksonville rock band the Noble Five, the boys considered long hair a professional necessity, although it violated the school's strict dress code. Gym teacher Leonard Skinner was the chief enforcer of the code, and generously doled out suspensions. Eventually the boys left school for good and the Noble Five became Lynyrd Skynyrd, named in honor of Lee High's push-up-dispensing educator.

McDuff Avenue runs north-south through western Jacksonville, off Interstate 10.

Miami

■ CEDARS OF LEBANON MEDICAL CENTER

1400 NW Twelfth Avenue, Miami

Reggae great Bob Marley died here, of cancer, in 1981.

Pan American Way, east of Bayshore Drive, Coconut Grove

Jim Morrison may or may not have exposed himself while onstage at the Coconut Grove's Dinner Key Auditorium in March 1969.

The Doors, winners of a University of Miami popularity contest, played for a beyond-capacity crowd of more than 10,000 fans that night. The concert started an hour late and was by all accounts an aesthetic disaster—Morrison guzzled from bottles handed up by audience members, stopped and restarted songs, and at one point was photographed holding a small lamb onstage. One of the show's promoters, fearing the crowd was out of hand, actually walked out from the wings and unplugged Robby Kreiger's guitar. A little later, a security guard threw Morrison from the stage. The *Miami Herald* reported the next day that the audience had included many "unescorted junior and senior high school girls."

Nobody in the band was arrested that night, but five audience members were detained (one of the arrests came when someone called a law enforcement officer a "pig"). The authorities later convicted Morrison on misdemeanor charges of profanity and public exposure. He died before serving any time.

Doors chroniclers speculate that Morrison's acts may have been inspired by an avant-garde theater piece he'd attended a few nights before in Los Angeles, where audience members were asked to strip themselves of their inhibitions, starting with their clothes. Perhaps those thoughts were still running through his mind when he took the stage at the Dinner Key. Band members and other witnesses claim they never saw Morrison fully expose himself and, by the standards of contemporary rock concerts, the only indecent thing Morrison did that night was perform a virtually incoherent show.

The Coconut Grove is just south of downtown Miami. Bayshore runs along the ocean, east of South Dixie Highway, and the Exhibition Center is northeast of the intersection of SW Twenty-seventh Avenue and Bayshore. Over the years, the auditorium has been enveloped by the expanding Exhibition Center, but the original Dinner Key space is marked by its checkerboard floor on the arena's east side.

1551 79th Street Causeway, Miami

arly in 1962 sisters Veronica and Estelle Bennett and cousin Nedra Talley lucked into work as go-go dancers at the famed Peppermint Lounge in New York City. They called themselves the Ronettes. Joey Dee and the Starlighters headlined the act, and the band occasionally let Veronica and the girls sing a number.

When the Starlighters relocated for a few weeks that spring to Miami's Peppermint Lounge—which would later give way to the Crab House—they took the Ronettes with them.

Vacationing in Miami at the time was New York disc jockey Murray the K. Murray met the Ronettes, liked the act, and invited them to appear on his radio show back home. Later, he got them a performing spot on one of his live rock 'n' roll revues. The Ronettes eventually came under the influence of master producer Phil Spector and recorded "Be My Baby," "Baby, I Love You," and many other hits. Veronica also married Phil.

The 79th Street causeway is attached to a major east-west route located four or five miles north of downtown Miami. The Crab House is still open, but unfortunately, according to local sources, the interior today looks nothing like it did during its twistin' years. The phone number is 305-868-7085.

■ CRITERIA STUDIOS

1755 NE 149th Street, Miami

azz buff and self-taught engineer Mack Emerman launched Criteria Studios in the late Fifties. Today, the complex has a half-dozen recording rooms and its own waterfall. Outside, it's a pretty nondescript cluster of buildings, but it's been one of America's leading producers of rock 'n' roll hit records for three decades. The waterfall, installed to calm the nerves of frazzled musicians, flows from the building's second story into an enclosed courtyard.

Criteria made its name in the Sixties and Seventies as a recording hub for Atlantic Records. The list of artists who have held sessions at Criteria runs from Abba to Zappa (and includes the Allman Brothers, Count Basie, Jimmy Buffett, Placido Domingo, Aretha Franklin, the Eagles, Fleetwood Mac, Bob

Marley, Little Richard, Ted Nugent, Wilson Pickett, the Rolling Stones, Ike and Tina Turner, and Neil Young).

It's no surprise that gold records adorn the lobby, including James Brown's "I Got You (I Feel Good)," Bob Seger's *Stranger in Town,* the Eagles' *Greatest Hits,* and hundreds of Bee Gees discs. Before they built their own studio, Criteria was the Bee Gees' recording headquarters. The *Saturday Night Fever* soundtrack (pre-*Thriller*, the best-selling rock album of all time) was made at Criteria. Eric Clapton was teamed with Duane Allman by producer Tom Dowd. As Derek and the Dominoes, they recorded *Layla and Other Assorted Love Songs* here.

■ THE DEAUVILLE HOTEL

6701 Collins Avenue, Miami Beach

On February 16, 1964, the Beatles' second appearance on "The Ed Sullivan Show" was broadcast from the Deauville Hotel's Napoleon Room, located just off the giant lobby. According to a review of the broadcast in the next morning's *Miami Herald,* Mitzi Gaynor stole the show.

Unfazed by the bad press, the Beatles spent the week following the performance lounging at the Deauville, running from Beatlemaniacs, and clowning on the beach. They also caught a Don Rickles floor show, visited Cassius Clay (who was training in Miami for his championship fight against Sonny Liston), attended their first drive-in movie (*Fun in Acapulco*), and cruised around the bay in a yacht. Miami Beach Police Sergeant Buddy Dresner, assigned to guard duty in the Beatles' suite, invited them home for a roast beef dinner one night. Later on that evening, the boys got loose with some local gals in the Deauville's Mau-Mau Lounge.

The Deauville is one of Collins Avenue's many faded beauties. Dance-band echoes still fill the air. Alas, the Mau-Mau Lounge, once located on the hotel's lower arcade, is no more. Call 305-865-8511 for reservations and more information.

4441 Collins Avenue, Miami Beach

In the days when fur and big cigars were standard equipment for a night on the town in Miami Beach, the Fontainebleau Hilton was the swingingest joint on the Atlantic seaboard. For a slice of Rat Pack swank, there is no better place east of Las Vegas Boulevard. The decor, the clientele, and the drink prices at the lobby bar may be unnerving, and the Fontainebleau could be considered an icon to values that rock 'n' roll has frequently sought to undermine, but the grand dowager remains a must-see for amateur sociologists visiting Miami.

Discounting the high jinks of Sammy, Joey, Dean, and Frank, the Fontainebleau has limited pop significance. Rock has never been particularly welcome in Miami's big hotels. There is, however, one event linked to this address that's worth mentioning. When Elvis Presley left the Army in 1960, he made his re-entry into popular consciousness by invading hostile territory: Miami Beach. Presley's first post-service television appearance was on a Frank Sinatra TV special, sponsored by Timex and broadcast live from the Fontainebleau's Grand Ballroom. Presley modeled his military uniform, did shtick with Joey Bishop, and sang a cornball duet with Sinatra himself. Judging from tapes of the special (brief excerpts are used in the movie *This Is Elvis*), the King's hair, piled several inches above his head, never looked better.

The reservations number is 305-538-2000.

6000 NW Seventh Avenue, Miami

The Sam and Dave duo was born at the King of Hearts Club in the mid-Fifties. The story goes that Sam (Moore) was working as amateur-night master of ceremonies at the club when Dave (Prater), a short-order cook still dressed in his chef's whites, jumped onstage and started to sing.

Since then, the club has been razed. It's now a parking lot.

■ SKYYWALKER STUDIO

67 NW 71st Street, Miami

In 1989, Luther Campbell and his 2 Live Crew cut their notorious rap album *As Nasty as They Wanna Be* at Skyywalker Studio. When the Crew found success, Skyywalker Records (since renamed Luke Records at the insistence of George Lucas' attorneys) set up offices in more upscale surroundings. But the studios are still here on 71st.

■ THE SUNNY ISLES BRIDGE

At State Highway 826, linking Miami and Miami Beach

In 1974, the Bee Gees crossed the Sunny Isles Bridge every evening en route to recording sessions at Criteria Studios. One night, Barry Gibb's wife, Linda, commented on the chunk-chunk-chunk sound the car's wheels made on the causeway. The group incorporated the rhythm into a tune called "Drive Talking," which they later renamed "Jive Talkin'." The song topped the charts and started a comeback for the Bee Gees.

■ T. K. PRODUCTIONS STUDIO

495 SE Tenth Court, Hialeah

Producer Henry Stone created quintessential Seventies disco at his T. K. Records studios. "Shake, Shake, Shake (Shake Your Booty)" and "Get Down Tonight" by KC and the Sunshine Band, "Rock Your Baby" by George McCrae, and "Clean Up Woman" by Betty Wright were recorded here, among many other disco classics.

The Tenth Court building has recently housed a wholesale clothing business. Drive north from the Miami International Airport on Highway 913 (sometimes called Le Jeune Road; other times called NE Eighth Avenue). Turn east on NE Eighth Avenue, onto 1st Street (in Miami called NW 54th Street), then north at NE Tenth Avenue. NE Tenth Court is near the intersection of NE Third Place and NE Tenth Avenue.

Orange Park

■ JACKSONVILLE MEMORY GARDENS

111 Blanding Boulevard, Orange Park

Ronnie Van Zant is entombed at Jacksonville Memory Gardens, not far from the graves of Steve and Cassie Gaines. These Lynyrd Skynyrd members all died in a tour-plane crash on October 20, 1977, near Gillsburg, Mississippi. According to cemetery attendants, Van Zant's mausoleum (inscribed with a reference to the band's anthem, "Free Bird") gets a steady stream of visitors.

Orange Park is a distant, southern suburb of Jacksonville. The cemetery is open 7 A.M. till dusk Monday through Friday; 9 A.M. to 3 P.M. on Saturday. The tomb and graves are right beside the cemetery office.

Orlando

■ THE HARD ROCK CAFE

5800 Kirkman Road, Orlando

The Orlando Hard Rock's collection includes instruments from all the members of U2, plus a Louis XVI stage costume once worn (smashingly) by Elton John. The building itself is quite a sight. The lot is shaped like a Fender Stratocaster, and the instrument's neck is the exit ramp off a highway. Three hundred feet long, the "neck" runs under a translucent roof laced with fiber-optic "strings" and is capped with huge silver "tuning pegs." The back door of the cafe opens onto the Universal Studios theme park. How could you stay away?

This Hard Rock serves, on average, 2,000–3,000 customers a day. Call 407-351-7625 for more information.

Orlando

■ SPACEPORT U.S.A./KENNEDY SPACE CENTER

On the Atlantic, east of Orlando, north of Cocoa Beach

In 1977, NASA sent Voyagers I and II into the depths of space loaded with essential information about Earth. Among the sounds etched into a gold-plated audio disc to be carried onboard was Chuck Berry's "Johnny B. Goode."

Drive east on the Beeline Expressway (Highway 528) from Orlando until you see "Spaceport, U.S.A." signs. Visitor-center hours usually run from 9 A.M. to 7 P.M., and tickets cost about $6. For more information, call 407-452-2121.

St. Augustine

■ THE FLORIDA SCHOOL FOR THE DEAF AND BLIND

207 North San Marco Avenue, St. Augustine

Ray Charles attended the Florida School for the Deaf and Blind from ages seven through fifteen (1937 through 1945). Here, he learned to read the Braille system of music notation and gained a reputation as a mischievous little man. For example, he once tried to drive a school maintenance truck across campus.

The campus is still a boarding and day school for 500 hearing- and vision-impaired students.

St. Petersburg

■ ST. PETERSBURG JUNIOR COLLEGE

6605 Fifth Avenue North, St. Petersburg

Jim Morrison and Tom Petty attended classes at St. Petersburg, although at different times. Morrison—who was already developing a personality during his stay here—liked to get drunk at dances and then stand in a corner pretending to be a tree. He later advanced to the Florida State University in Tallahassee and film school at UCLA.

GEORGIA

Athens

■ THE EPISCOPAL CHURCH

394 Oconee Street, Athens

The early Eighties were a big time for Athens. Old hands like the B-52s had been playing around town since 1977, and Pylon, Love Tractor, and the tadpole version of R.E.M. all began flaunting alternative poses to the prevailing preppie, jock, and redneck ones around the University of Georgia campus.

The group that would become R.E.M. first performed April 5, 1980, at a birthday party in a broken-down, abandoned Episcopal church on Oconee Street, playing oldies till dawn. (In fact, in those days the group, although born of the university's art school crowd, was scorned for only doing cover tunes.)

Guitarist Peter Buck and vocalist Michael Stipe actually resided in the church for about nine months; bassist Mike Mills and drummer Bill Berry occasionally crashed here, too.

The only part of the church now remaining is its steeple, easily visible at the intersection of Oglethorpe and Oconee streets. The steeple is now incorporated into a condominium development. R.E.M's members all still live in Athens and are active in local politics.

■ THE 40 WATT CLUB

256 West Clayton Street, Athens

The old 40 Watt Club at West Clayton Street was a prime performance spot for all the important Athens bands in the late Seventies and early Eighties. The 256 West Clayton address is currently a T-shirt factory. The 40 Watt now operates (and the next generation of Athens bands toils) at 285 West Washington Street, where the phone number is 404-549-7871.

■ THE MORTON THEATER

199 West Washington Street, Athens

The B-52s rehearsed in the back of the old Morton Theater, which dates from the vaudeville era and was once a center of black culture in Athens. According to legend, the theater abutted an old mortuary and the band's rehearsal space was the place's bloodletting room.

The theater still stands, and is currently being renovated.

■ WUXTRY RECORDS

197 East Clayton Street, Athens

Peter Buck was a clerk at the downtown outlet of Wuxtry Records. Michael Stipe happened in as a customer one day, and soon Buck was setting aside the latest punk albums for him. From that meeting came R.E.M. The rest is history.

Wuxtry is still in business, at several locations around town.

Atlanta

■ FOX THEATRE

660 Peachtree Street NE, Atlanta

The Fox Theatre, a virtual palace in the Oriental style, opened on Christmas 1929, and has since been host to almost every musical performer. Elvis Presley played the Fox in 1956, and Jimmy Buffett and Lynyrd Skynyrd recorded big-selling live albums here in the Seventies.

In addition to concerts, the Fox stages a full schedule of theater and musical-comedy productions. Call 404-881-2100 for more information.

■ FUNOCHIO'S

845 Peachtree Street NE, Atlanta

Al Kooper, producer, musician, and owner of Sounds of the South Records (an offshoot of MCA), discovered Lynyrd Skynyrd during one of the band's stands at Funochio's, an Atlanta club. After joining the group in a jam session, Kooper signed them to the label.

The 845 Peachtree building now houses Backstreet Atlanta, a gay club.

■ GREAT SOUTHEAST MUSIC HALL AND EMPORIUM

3871 Peachtree Road NE, Brookhaven

The late Great Southeast Music Hall was one of the liveliest and unlikeliest homes of punk rock in America. The Sex Pistols opened their first and only American tour with a concert here on January 5, 1978. Peter Buck, future R.E.M. guitarist, crashed the gates but was thrown out after one song. Later that year, Atlanta's first Punk Festival, headlined by the B-52s, was held here.

Part of a suburban shopping center called Cherokee Plaza, the hall itself is gone. A dentist's office and a drugstore now occupy its shell.

Macon

■ DUANE ALLMAN CRASH SITE

Bartlett Street and Hillcrest Avenue, Macon

Duane Allman crashed his motorcycle at the Bartlett Street/Hillcrest Avenue intersection at dusk on October 29, 1971, while trying to avoid a flatbed trailer truck. Allman, lead guitarist for the Allman Brothers Band and virtuoso accompanist on records by Eric Clapton and Otis Redding, died three hours later at Middle Georgia Medical Center.

Exit Interstate 75 at Mercer University Boulevard and drive west to Pio Nono Avenue (Highway 41). Take that north to Napier Avenue, go west to Inverness, north to Hillcrest, and west to Bartlett.

One year and two weeks after Allman's wreck, the band's bassist Berry Oakley died in a similar accident at the intersection of Napier Avenue and Inverness Street, just two blocks south of Allman's crash site.

■ THE "BIG HOUSE"

2321 Vineville Avenue, Macon

In the early years, Allman Brothers Band members lived communally at the "Big House" at 2321 Vineville. Duane Allman attended a birthday party here the evening he died.

■ H & H RESTAURANT

807 Forsyth Street, Macon

"Mama" Louise Hudson, owner of H & H Restaurant, was one of the Allman Brothers Band's first fans. She was also their guardian and benefactor, seeing that the boys were fed in the early, poor days. She still presides over H & H (specializing in soul food and Southern cooking), and photos and a mural depicting Duane Allman and Berry Oakley as angels strumming guitars celebrate the restaurant's role in ABB history.

Just down the street, at 536 Broadway, is the building that housed Capricorn Records, the band's recording studio. The company's logo is still visible above the door.

■ MACON CITY AUDITORIUM

415 1st Street, Macon

Approximately 8,000 people jammed the Macon City Auditorium to attend Otis Redding's funeral in 1967, including Aretha Franklin, James Brown, Stevie Wonder, and Wilson Pickett. Joe South sang.

In earlier, happier days, the hall had been the setting for Little Richard Penniman's first professional singing engagement. Little Richard, who grew up at 1540 Fifth Avenue in Macon, sang on a bill topped by Sister Rosetta Tharpe; he was twelve.

Call 404-751-9250 for more information on the auditorium.

■ OTIS REDDING MEMORIAL BRIDGE

Martin Luther King Jr. Boulevard, Macon

Otis Redding, a native of nearby Dawson, grew up in Macon. He died in a plane crash in 1967. Macon's memorial to him, a bridge spanning the Ocmulgee River, was dedicated in 1974 to "a native son, singer, composer and performer." He was headed for superstardom at the time of his death.

Redding is buried on his family's private ranch (The Big O) outside of town. Neither the grave nor the ranch is open to the public.

■ ROSE HILL CEMETERY

Off Interstate 75, Macon

A beautiful, historic cemetery, Rose Hill holds several landmarks dear to Allman Brothers fans. The graveyard was something of a haunt for the band in its early days, and its markers and monuments inspired songs and album jackets. Now, two of the founding members are buried here.

Mourners pay their last respects to Otis Redding (Macon, Georgia)

The stone that inspired the song "In Memory of Elizabeth Reed" is at the northern perimeter of the cemetery, near the Ocmulgee River; a marker in the Hawthorne Ridge section of the cemetery sparked the idea for the song "Little Martha." The back cover of the band's eponymous first album carries a photo shot at Rose Hill's Overlook Monument, located in the far-northwest corner of the grounds.

Guitarist Duane Allman and bassist Berry Oakley are buried side by side at the top of Rose Hill's Carnation Ridge. Both men died in Macon, in motorcycle accidents just two blocks apart—Allman in October 1971, Oakley in November 1972.

Oakley's marker is inscribed: "Help thy brother's boat across / And, lo! thine own has reached the shore." Etched into the monument elsewhere are the words ". . . and the road goes on forever . . ."

Allman's headstone, often surrounded by gifts from fans (flowers, guitar picks, beer bottles), is inscribed with drawings of a Les Paul guitar, the musical notes of "Little Martha," and mushrooms, a band symbol. It also carries some Allman-penned poetry:

> *I love being alive and I will be the best man*
> *I possibly can. I will take love wherever*
> *I find it and offer it to everyone who will*
> *Take it . . . seek knowledge from those wiser*
> *And teach those who wish to learn from me.*

The cemetery is on the Ocmulgee River, just east of Interstate 75, and is open dawn to dusk. The phone number is 912-751-9119.

■ THE WELCOME CENTER

200 Cherry Street, Macon

Macon has a unique affection for the musicians who have called the town home. There's the Otis Redding bridge and a Little Richard boulevard. In the old railroad station that houses the Macon-Bibb County Convention and Visitors Bureau there's the Welcome Center, which not only offers music-oriented maps and guides, but also has an on-staff specialist in Macon's musical

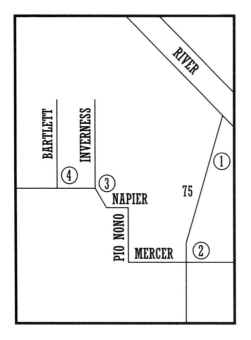

*A few of Macon's many, many
cool sites:*
1) Rose Hill Cemetery
2) Little Richard Penniman Road
3) Berry Oakley crash site
4) Duane Allman crash site

history, R. Martin Willett. Rock 'n' roll pilgrims are strongly advised to check in with Willett when planning a visit to Macon. (Some day, every city will have staff people devoted to this kind of history.) The Center's even set up a toll-free number: 800-768-3401.

■ WIBB RADIO

830 Mulberry Street, Macon

A pioneering black radio station, WIBB is still a powerful force in that market, and helps sponsor Macon's big street parties every spring and fall. In 1952, James Brown was nineteen and had just been released from the prison at Toccoa. He eventually made his way to Macon and struggled along playing in local nightclubs. But in November 1955 he came to WIBB's sound studio on Mulberry Street to record "Please, Please, Please." And soon, his career began to churn.

The station has since moved, and is now at 369 2nd Street.

LOUISIANA

Ferriday

■ HANEY'S BIG HOUSE

E. E. Wallace Boulevard, Ferriday

Haney's Big House closed a few decades ago, but until then it was Ferriday's biggest black club. In its prime it stretched for half a block and entertained the cream of the South's touring blues acts—Sunnyland Slim, Big Maceo, Roy Milton, Memphis Slim, and others.

The club earned its place in rock history in the late Forties, when local teens Jerry Lee Lewis and his cousin Jimmy Lee Swaggart began sneaking away from home and riding their bicycles down to the bar. At Haney's, young Jimmy and Jerry were exposed to music far more vivid than what they were hearing at the local Assembly of God church. Still, the club was a comparatively positive distraction: when the boys weren't absorbing barrelhouse piano tricks at Haney's, they were robbing stores downtown.

Lewis soaked up a lot of soul at Haney's and turned it into his own thumping boogie-woogie style. Swaggart took the high road, establishing a popular television ministry, although temptation continues to dog him.

Ferriday is just across the Mississippi from Natchez. Haney's is a vacant lot now, located on Highway 65, Ferriday's main street (locals call it E. E. Wallace Boulevard) just north of the Unique Club and Charlie's Lounge. The bar called Big Boy's supposedly stands on the rear part of Haney's foundation.

Natchitoches

■ JIM CROCE DEATH SITE

Natchitoches Airport, Natchitoches

Jim Croce died in a plane crash at Natchitoches Airport on September 20, 1973. He had just completed a concert at Prather Coliseum, the basketball arena at Northwestern State University. The group's small charter plane took off toward the south, veered off the runway's center line about halfway down the strip, then hit the trees east of the runway.

Natchitoches is off Interstate 49. The airport is located on the bypass highway that rings the town.

New Orleans

■ THE DEW DROP INN

2836 LaSalle Street, New Orleans

The Dew Drop Inn apparently began as a barber shop, but it evolved into a bar and restaurant *and* the premiere black nightclub in New Orleans. Most of the major jazz and blues stars played the Inn over the years, but its place in rock history was assured by what supposedly happened one September night in 1955. New Orleans recording studio owner Cosimo Matassa disputes the tale, but legend has it that during a break from a session at Matassa's, Little Richard Penniman came in for a few drinks. The session, one of Penniman's first, wasn't going well, and his producers thought a respite would do everyone some good. Spying the Dew Drop's piano, the frustrated Penniman began pounding out a bawdy song about "good booty." Local songwriter Dorothy La Bostrie was quickly drafted to write decent lyrics—"Tutti Frutti, aw rootie!"— and Little Richard had his first hit for Specialty Records.

The Dew Drop Inn closed in the early Seventies and is now boarded up, although the building still stands.

■ THE HARD ROCK CAFE

418 North Peters Street, New Orleans

In addition to the standard gold records and guitars (including one once played by Jimmy Page), this Hard Rock Cafe in the French Quarter has gone for indigenous collectibles: a piece of Fats Domino's piano, a hat and cane from Dr. John, a Clifton Chenier accordion, jackets worn by Allen Toussaint and Professor Longhair, and a full Mardi Gras parade costume worn by the Wild Tchoupitoulas.

Call 504-529-5617 for more information.

Jazz at Ground Zero

Rock 'n' Roll was made from pieces of blues, country, gospel, hillbilly—even jazz. The rompin', stompin', brand of pioneering jazz made in New Orleans now seems well removed from rock, but without it, rock would never have learned to swing.

■ **CONGO SQUARE**

Before the Civil War, black slaves were allowed to mingle on Sunday afternoons (their only time off) at New Orleans' Congo Square, where there would be wild tom-tom playing and African dancing. Although whites feared that the movements and music were making voodoo magic, historians say that what was really being created was rudimentary jazz.

The place is now called Beauregard Square, and is located in the southwestern corner of Louis Armstrong Park.

■ **LOUIS ARMSTRONG PARK**
North Rampart and St. Ann Streets

No other single person better symbolizes the best of twentieth-century American music than the fellow commemorated by the statue in this park. A brilliant and innovative improviser and cornet player, he's the guy who, when asked for a definition of jazz, replied: "If you have to ask, you'll never know."

■ **STORYVILLE**
North of Basin Street, near the French Quarter

Some musicologists credit Storyville as the true birthplace of jazz. This zoning-experiment-gone-mad was New Orleans' legal red light district for about twenty years around the turn of the century, and many early jazz stars were employed as entertainers in the bad/good houses of Storyville. The district was so much fun (or so wicked) that the Secretary of the Navy ordered it shut down in 1917.

This area, located north of Basin Street near the French Quarter, is now near the Iverville housing project, another zoning experiment.

■ J & M STUDIOS

North Rampart, Gov. Nichols, and Camp Streets, New Orleans

L egendary recording engineer Cosimo Matassa was present at most (if not all) of the greatest moments in New Orleans rock 'n' roll history. He ran several recording studios around town, and each one saw legends being made.

Matassa owned a record store at 838 North Rampart Street and set up his first studio in the back room. Professor Longhair came here to record, as did Dave Bartholomew and the incomparable Fats Domino.

Matassa then built studios at 521 and 523 Gov. Nichols Street, and used 525 for offices and mastering. (523 and 525 are basically one structure—an old hospital. 521 had been a private house.) Little Richard cut his biggest hits, including "Tutti Frutti," "Rip It Up," "Lucille," and "Good Golly Miss Molly," in the studio at 523. Clarence "Frog Man" Henry recorded "Ain't Got No Home" and Lee Dorsey made "Ya Ya" in the same space. Now 521 is a house again, and the others are condominiums.

In 1964, Matassa moved to the second floor of 748 Camp Street. Two years later, Aaron Neville came here to record "Tell It Like It Is." The space is no longer used as a studio.

New Orleans is contemplating restoring one or more of Matassa's studios, but as of now none is open.

■ PROFESSOR LONGHAIR'S GRAVE

Mount Olivet Cemetery, 4000 Norman Mayers Road, New Orleans

A lthough at the time of his death in January 1980 Professor Longhair— Henry Roeland Byrd—was gaining popularity, he'd lived most of his life in relative obscurity around New Orleans. The Professor's swinging piano style, as adapted by Fats Domino, Huey "Piano" Smith, and others, had a pervasive influence on early rock 'n' roll. When he played, all of New Orleans came out of his fingertips.

The cemetery's office hours are 8:30 A.M. to 5 P.M. daily, and the phone number is 504-283-4358.

■ TIPITINA'S

501 Napoleon Avenue, New Orleans

Although it's not one of New Orleans' ancient landmarks (it was founded in the late Seventies), Tipitina's (named after the Professor Longhair tune) has nonetheless become the city's most prominent space for the performance of hometown funk and rock 'n' roll. The local zydeco bands, the Neville Brothers, Dr. John, and others play here frequently. Professor Longhair—whose left hand has influenced anybody who ever has or will play rock 'n' roll piano—performed here, too.

Call 504-895-8477 for information.

MISSISSIPPI

The Delta

■ THE DELTA BLUES MUSEUM

114 Delta Avenue, Clarksdale

Seemingly a logical place to start a Delta Blues pilgrimage, the Delta Blues Museum is not in that kind of shape—yet. But there are some highlights, including a life-size dummy of Muddy Waters, a few old records, *and* the Muddywood guitar. This is an oddly beautiful instrument made from a plank torn from Waters' house on nearby Stovall Plantation. Muddywood was commissioned by ZZ Top as a fund-raising device for the museum.

The museum is on the top floor of Clarksdale's old Carnegie Library. Hours—typically about 10 A.M. to 4:30 P.M.—don't always coincide with library hours, and may change by the season. Call 601-624-4461.

Memphis and Points South

Celebrated in song by Bob Dylan, Highway 61 linked South to North—New Orleans through Memphis to St. Louis, Chicago, and Detroit. Via Highway 61 and the Illinois Central Railroad, rural acoustic blues rode up from the Delta to the industrial North, became amplified, and turned into rock 'n' roll.

One outfit making that epic trek, back in 1951, was Ike Turner and His Kings of Rhythm. Ike, just eighteen, was up from Clarksdale and headed for Memphis with his band. The group's sedan, overloaded with black teenagers, guitars, and drums, shed a bit of its cargo onto Highway 61. It was a guitar amp, and it got busted and squashed. The band tossed the cabinet back on board and pressed on toward Sun Studio, where studio owner Sam Phillips attempted to repair the speaker by stuffing paper into its cone. Once attached to a guitar, the resulting sound was nothing but a nasty buzz. The group used that amp on a rollicking road song called "Rocket 88" (sung by Ike's sax player, Jackie Brenston). Sam Phillips himself says it's the first real rock 'n' roll record.

Other tales of Highway 61:

In September 1937, Bessie Smith, the *first* first lady of the blues, died from injuries suffered during an auto accident on the Highway, near Coahoma.

As mentioned earlier, the intersection of Highway 61 and Highway 49, near the center of Clarksdale, is generally considered the crossroads at which Robert Johnson traded his soul to the Devil for that dazzling guitar-picking technique.

The mythology gets thick down in blues country. Before jumping to any hasty conclusions, however, nonbelievers should drive Highway 61 through the Delta at night, then stand at a crossroads alone for a while.

■ **STACKHOUSE/DELTA RECORD MART**

---

232 Sunflower Avenue, Clarksdale

Home base for Jim O'Neal and *Living Blues* magazine, Stackhouse/Delta Record Mart offers the definitive Delta tour packet, a necessity for any total-immersion blues trip through the South. O'Neal also offers his blues kit via mail order, and $7.50 will bring maps, a delightfully unromantic overview of the area's dozens of relevant blues landmarks, and even a few tips on juke-joint etiquette.

The shop also carries records, CDs, tapes, and lots of reading material. Hours are irregular, but tend to be from noon to dinnertime. Call 601-627-2209 for more information or to order your Delta Blues Map Kit.

■ STOVALL PLANTATION

Oakhurst Avenue, outside Clarksdale

Muddy Waters (McKinley Morganfield) grew up on Stovall Plantation and made his early living driving a tractor (for 22.5 cents an hour) and selling whiskey on the side. At the age of 26 he was discovered by Library of Congress folk-song collectors who were in the area looking for Robert Johnson. Johnson, by this time, had died, so they recorded Waters instead, right in his house, which doubled as a juke joint for plantation workers. Soon, Muddy was en route to Chicago.

The Delta Blues Museum in Clarksdale, home of the Muddywood guitar, is considering setting up the rest of Waters' house as a display.

The plantation is on Oakhurst Avenue, about seven miles northwest of Clarksdale.

Gillsburg

■ LYNYRD SKYNYRD CRASH SITE

Off Highway 568, near Gillsburg

The prop-driven Convair 240 carrying Ronnie Van Zant and Steve and Cassie Gaines of Lynyrd Skynyrd, along with 23 others, crashed outside Gillsburg on October 20, 1977. Six of the passengers died that night, including Van Zant and the Gaineses. The band was traveling between Greenville, South Carolina, and Baton Rouge, Louisiana. The plane was low on fuel and had been directed to the McComb, Mississippi, airport for an emergency landing, but went down about eight miles southwest of the McComb airport in a swampy, heavily wooded area. The first rescue workers to the scene had to cross a twenty-foot-wide stream to get to the wreckage. Later, a road was bulldozed to the site. The whole evacuation took three hours.

Not even people who assisted in the rescue remember the exact location of the wreck. According to National Transportation Safety Board records, the precise latitude and longitude of the fuselage when it was found were 31 degrees, 4 minutes, and 19 seconds/90 degrees, 35 minutes, and 57 seconds. The site is unmarked.

Meridian

■ PEAVEY MELODY MUSIC

813 Twenty-second Avenue, Meridian

J B. Peavey opened a record and musical instrument store in Meridian in 1946. Ten years later, his teenage son, Hartley, saw Bo Diddley play and begged for a guitar and an amp. When his father wouldn't come through, Hartley designed an amp of his own, and thus was born the Peavey Electronics empire. Today the Peavey company, which earned its reputation making public-address systems and guitar (especially bass guitar) amplifiers, is one of America's leading manufacturers of rock 'n' roll instruments. The old music store is no longer owned by the Peavey family, but still carries many guitars. Call 601-483-9215 for hours.

The Peavey manufacturing company is still based in Meridian, at 711 A Street. Meridian also has a museum devoted to the life and works of Hartley Peavey in the Northeast Industrial Park on Marion Russell Road. The museum, built into an old agriculture experiment station in 1991, features a re-creation of the basement workshop where young Hartley first experimented with amplification. There's also a demo room in which Peavey instruments are available for tour takers to play and a gift shop that carries a full line of clothing and other goods marked with the distinctive Peavey logo (designed by Hartley himself while doodling during a high-school class). The museum is free; it's open 10 A.M. to 4 P.M. weekdays and weekend afternoons. Call 601-483-5365 for more information.

Morgan City

■ ROBERT JOHNSON MEMORIAL

Mount Zion Church Graveyard, Highway 7, near Morgan City

The "King of the Delta Blues Singers" may or may not be buried in Morgan City. Robert Johnson died in 1938. Poisoned by a jealous husband, he lingered for days in agony and, according to legend, howled like a dog during his last hours. Today, his music continues to influence guitarists and blues singers. (A boxed set of his recordings topped the charts in 1991.)

No small part of Johnson's appeal is tied to the mystery that surrounds his short life, and his final resting place is as perplexing as the rest of the story. According to his death certificate, Johnson was buried at the Mount Zion graveyard, a few feet from the Mount Zion Church. Although some evidence contradicts the death certificate, Columbia Records paid for a marker at Mount Zion in the spring of 1991. It is a hauntingly beautiful obelisk, inscribed with song lyrics and usually surrounded by offerings from fans.

Even if Johnson is buried in Mount Zion, the stone does not mark the exact location of his grave, which has never been identified. If he is buried elsewhere, one possible site is the Payne Baptist Church in nearby Quito. There's a memorial for him there, too.

To get to Mount Zion, take Highway 82 eight miles west from Greenwood, Mississippi, then turn south on Highway 7. The chapel will come up in

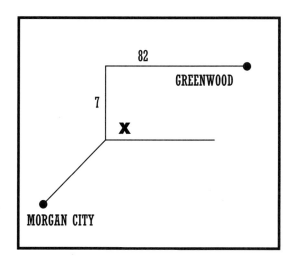

The Robert Johnson memorial

just over ten miles. Quito and the Payne Baptist Church are a few miles north on Highway 7.

Tupelo

■ ELVIS PRESLEY BIRTHPLACE COMPLEX

306 Elvis Presley Drive, Tupelo

Elvis Presley's birthplace is a tiny white house—locals call it a shotgun shack because a shot fired through the front doorway would go straight out the back. Now restored, it's in a Tupelo city park and can be toured for a small donation.

A pleasant gift shop sits just up the hill from the shack; a playground that Presley helped launch with a 1957 benefit concert is farther up. Also nearby is a chapel—one of the oddest attractions in all of Elvis Country. On display there are one of Elvis' personal Bibles and the pulpit from Tupelo's First Assembly of God church, where the Presley family supposedly worshipped. But the chapel's centerpiece is a large stained-glass window: Is that a white bird taking flight at the center of the glass, or is it Elvis himself, spreading the wings of his jumpsuit?

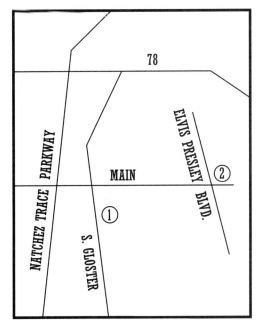

Tupelo landmarks:
1) The Elvis McDonald's
2) The Elvis birthplace

The complex also has a museum, which will be the official repository of the 3,000-piece Elvis memorabilia collection of local fan Janelle McComb.

Tupelo is 102 miles southeast of Memphis and the birthplace complex is a mile east of central Tupelo, just north of East Main Street. The Presley home, visitors' center and chapel are open year-round. The hours are 9 A.M. to about 5:30 P.M. Monday through Saturday, and 1 P.M. to 5 P.M. Sunday. Call 601-841-1245.

■ ELVIS MCDONALD'S

372 South Gloster Street, Tupelo

The Gloster Street McDonald's is not your typical franchise. Janelle Mc-Comb, an Elvis fan and Presley family friend, has put part of her vast private collection of Elvis memorabilia on display here. Also eye-catching are the etched-glass window portraits of You Know Who, which act as room dividers between the service counter and the seating area.

This somewhat surreal landmark is situated across the street from Tupelo Mall.

TENNESSEE

Memphis

■ AMERICAN SOUND STUDIOS

827 Danny Thomas Boulevard, Memphis

Producer Chips Moman opened American Sound Studios in the mid-Sixties and immediately set about making hits, a few of which are "The Letter," "Soul Deep," and "Cry Like a Baby" by the Box Tops; "Hooked on a Feeling" and "I Just Can't Help Believing" by B. J. Thomas; "Son of a Preacher Man" by Dusty Springfield; "Skinny Legs and All" and "I Gotcha" by Joe Tex; and "Keep On Dancing" by the Gentrys.

In January and February 1969 Elvis Presley came here for the *From Elvis*

Elvis Presley Park (Tupelo)

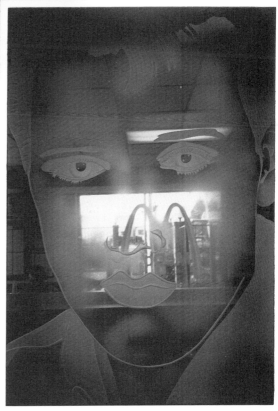

The Elvis McDonald's (Tupelo)

in Memphis sessions and produced "Kentucky Rain," "In the Ghetto," and "Suspicious Minds."

A Chief Auto Parts store occupies a whole new building where American once stood, on the northwest corner of Chelsea and Thomas.

■ **ARDENT STUDIOS**

2000 Madison Avenue, Memphis

One of the South's premiere modern recording facilities, Ardent has played host to R.E.M., Stevie Ray Vaughan, Robert Cray, the Allman Brothers Band, the Fabulous Thunderbirds, the Replacements, and others. ZZ Top made all of its Eighties' hits here.

Members of the public are sometimes allowed to tour the complex, but only in the morning and at the discretion of the staff.

■ **BEALE STREET**

East of Front, south of Union, and north of Linden Streets, Memphis

For most of the twentieth century, Beale Street was the center for black culture in Memphis, the heart of the city's music scene, and occasionally a dangerous—even murderous—place. Urban renewal swept through in the Seventies, and the small historic district that remains is neat—perhaps too neat. Memphians had hoped they could turn Beale into a Bourbon Street North tourist mecca. That hasn't happened yet, but the few shops, bars, and restaurants on the row are decent places and fairly popular with tourists, and the live music at night has started to attract locals as well.

Rock 'n' roll walked right up Beale Street on its way from the Mississippi Delta to Chicago. Historical markers along the street designate various current and former places of interest. Some highlights are:

- Pee-wee's Saloon at 209 Beale—about midway up the street—was demolished long ago. W. C. Handy, credited with being the first person to successfully mine the blues idiom for commercial success, frequented Pee-wee's and, according to legend, penned "Memphis Blues" there.

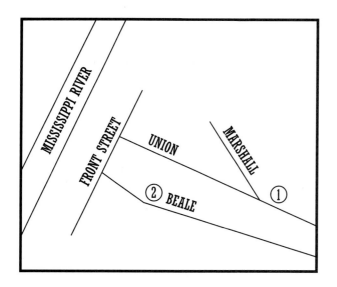

Downtown Memphis:
1) Sun Studios
2) Beale Street

- A. Schwab's (163 Beale) is a fine oddball attraction, a general store that opened in 1876 and apparently hasn't changed since.
- B. B. King's Blues Club (143 Beale) opened in May 1991, and everyone here hopes the addition of this big name will get the street up and running. Food is served, the music is usually good, and B. B. himself plays occasionally.
- The Center for Southern Folklore (152 Beale) moved to the street in 1989. This is the place to see thoughtful displays and exhibits on the area's heritage, including its music. Ask about the Center's walking tours of Beale, or call 901-525-3655 for more information.
- Handy Park, featuring a statue of W. C. himself, is at one end of the street.
- The Elvis Presley Statue, dedicated in August 1980, stands at the other end. The nine-foot-tall bronze, said to be one of the most-photographed sites in Memphis, has suffered considerable wear and tear at the hands of fans.
- Across the street from the Elvis statue is the former site of the Lansky Brothers clothing store (126 Beale), which for years advertised itself as "outfitter to the King." And it's true: Elvis bought a lot of his early onstage wardrobe here. During his later concert period, when he favored flashy jumpsuits onstage, Elvis continued to shop at Lansky's for his offstage look. Lansky's closed in summer

Beale Street, when it was the center of black culture in Memphis (Memphis, Tennessee)

1990, although the company still runs stores around the area under various names. The old building's west wall carries a large mural dedicated to Memphis history and Elvis' place in it, and is also much-photographed by tourists.

- Beale has its own little Walk of Fame, featuring musical notes imbedded in the sidewalk.
- The Rum Boogie Cafe (182 Beale) is the street's busiest music club and has been almost since its 1985 opening. Guitars of the stars (including donations from Eurythmic Dave Stewart, Willie Dixon, Stevie Ray Vaughan, Albert Collins, and many local players) and other music memorabilia are displayed around the cafe's interior. Live music is featured at night, and hearty Southern food is served round the clock. Best of all, the old Stax recording studio sign, rescued from the marquee above the studio's entrance, is displayed over the stage.

Beale Street is busiest in the summer season, when free live music often can be heard in the parks and on the sidewalks. Call 901-576-8171 for more information.

■ THE FULL GOSPEL TABERNACLE

787 Hale Road, Whitehaven

The pastor of the Full Gospel Tabernacle is the Reverend Al Green. Green, who created sweet soul music in the early Seventies, later abandoned secular sounds to serve God. Today his preaching is described as quite hot, and he frequently breaks into song, backed by a full soul combo and choir. In the past, a guide to religious rites peculiar to this church—including "prophecy of tongues" and "singing in the Spirit"—has been included with each program handed out at services.

Hale Road intersects Highway 51 (Elvis Presley Boulevard) just a few blocks south of Graceland; drive west from there. Services begin at 10:45 A.M. on Sunday, and visitors are welcome. But be warned that the Reverend Green's appearances at the church are sporadic. Call 901-396-9192.

Elvisville

Elvis is everywhere, of course, but he is especially so in Memphis. (It's likely that the locals who aren't cashing in on the King would prefer to forget his parents ever moved here.) No matter where you go in greater Memphis, he is inescapable, and moments from his life dot the landscape. A driving tour of Elvisville would have to include these landmarks:

■ **BAPTIST MEMORIAL HOSPITAL**
899 Madison Avenue

During the last few years of his life, Elvis checked in and out of Baptist Memorial Hospital several times and for a variety of reasons. He was officially pronounced dead here in August 1977.

The site is not totally associated with sadness, though. Lisa Marie Presley was born at Baptist Memorial in February 1968.

■ **FAIRGROUNDS AMUSEMENT PARK**
940 Early Maxwell Boulevard

The Fairgrounds Amusement Park is now called Libertyland. Elvis would rent the park (for $14,000 a night) to throw parties and ride the Zippin' Pippin roller coaster.

■ **HUMES HIGH SCHOOL**
659 North Manassas Street

Elvis had just entered his teens when the Presley family moved to Memphis, where he became a member of the Humes High graduating class of 1953. The school, which is now a junior high, has remade one classroom into an Elvis mini-museum, and the auditorium has been dedicated to the school's most famous alumnus.

■ LAUDERDALE COURTS
185 Winchester Street

The Lauderdale Courts was one of the early Presley family residences following the big move up from Mississippi. It was, and is, a public housing project. No shrines, and no accommodations have been made for Elvis cultists.

■ THE MEMPHIAN THEATER
51 South Cooper Street

Elvis liked to rent the Memphian Theater (now called Playhouse on the Square) for private late-night movie screenings.

Information about organized bus tours of some of these places may be obtained at Graceland. The phone number is 901-332-3322.

■ GRACELAND

3764 Elvis Presley Boulevard, Memphis

Graceland, Elvis Presley's final home, stands on the original site of a 500-acre farm owned in the nineteenth century by the Toof family. (One of the Toofs was named Grace, and a descendant of Grace's built the mansion in 1939.) Elvis paid $100,000 in cash for the house and the 13.8 acres surrounding it in 1957, when he was 22. Twenty years later he was found dead in an upstairs bathroom.

Graceland and its surrounding attractions first opened for tours in 1982. Today, visitors board a van at a bustling staging area at the bottom of the hill, drive across Elvis Presley Boulevard, pass the ornate front gates, and unload at the door. Then, in small groups, they're led through Elvis' house, past the huge living-room couch, many TV sets, and the Jungle Room. They see the backyard, the racquetball building, the trophy room, and the family burial plot out by the pool. The tour guides say that Graceland has become the second-most-visited residence in America, bested only by the White House. But only Graceland has that pink Cadillac.

Guides like to point out that Graceland is still a functioning domicile. Elvis' aunt, Delta Biggs, has lived here since 1967, in apartment-sized quarters near the back. She also uses the kitchen. Aunt Biggs' presence gives the place a

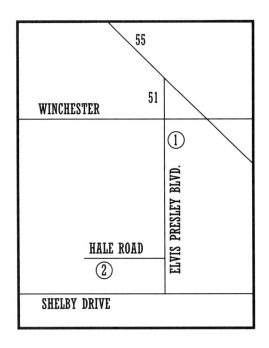

The sites of South Memphis:
1) Graceland
2) Al Green's Full Gospel
Tabernacle

lived-in feel, which is a little spooky, but it also adds immeasurably to the tour's impact. The first groups through the house in the morning sometimes get a whiff of Aunt Biggs' breakfast bacon cooking.

The pink Alabama fieldstone wall and the famed front gate that separate Graceland proper from the rest of the world have their own place in rock 'n' roll lore. After a Memphis concert on April 29, 1976, Bruce Springsteen, hoping to meet his idol, jumped the wall here but was told Elvis was out of town. Later that same year, Jerry Lee Lewis announced himself (by running his Lincoln Continental into the gate) and insisted on an audience with the King. When met with resistance from a guard, Lewis said, "You just tell him the Killer's here." The Memphis police were on the scene shortly and, discovering that the Killer was packing a .38 Derringer, took him away in handcuffs. Today, the wall functions as an unofficial guest book. Consider spending some quality time here, reading the personal ads to Elvis.

Some key parts of the house, including the kitchen and all the upstairs bedrooms and bathrooms, are off-limits to tourists. Elvis had an office up there, a dressing room, the master bedroom (King-sized bed with two TV sets recessed into the ceiling above it, ceiling otherwise padded in gold-glitter tufted vinyl) and a nursery for Lisa Marie. The upstairs rooms remain exactly as they were on the day Elvis left the building for good.

Messages to the King (Graceland, 1992)

The Trophy Room, an outbuilding erected as a place for Elvis to race his slot-car collection, is spectacular. Corporate Graceland has redesigned it as a display area for memorabilia and photos: see Elvis' gun collection, his jewelry, his stage costumes (including the leather outfit from his 1968 comeback TV special), Priscilla's wedding dress, and more. In fact, the most impressive area on the whole tour is easily the Hall of Gold, located in the Trophy Room. There are more than 200 gold and platinum albums on these walls. Cynics who have spent the tour disparaging Elvis' interior-design vision usually get very quiet here.

There are no large gaudy billboards announcing Graceland's presence to the approaching motorist. There *is* a very large jet airliner parked across the street from the mansion, however, negating the need for elaborate signage. As everyone knows, Elvis had a couple of airplanes and a bus, and these are parked beside the staging area and can be toured.

A car museum is at the south end of the staging area, and this building is a must-see. Elvis' various vehicles are here, some spinning on turntables. Here is where they keep the pink Cadillac—the one Elvis bought for his mother. The centerpiece of the car room is an area made to resemble a little drive-in theater, where visitors can screen excerpts from Elvis movies. The gift shop you pass through after the car museum has a special display tree full of Elvis' heavy-metal trademark sun goggles. There's just one style here—E-style. Meanwhile, Elvis music plays continuously over the public-address system.

Elvis, his father Vernon, mother Gladys, and aunt Minnie Mae are all buried in the Meditation Garden, which Elvis built in the mid-Sixties. The King wasn't planning on spending eternity here at the time; he just wanted a quiet place to think. His body was originally buried at Forest Hill Cemetery, just down the road, as was his mother's. But security there became a concern, and Vernon decided to move his son and Gladys home. Now there's an eternal flame at the grave site, a fountain, benches, stained glass, and lots of contemplative friends of Elvis'.

Graceland is rock 'n' roll's number one tourist attraction, no question about it, and so far the *only* rock landmark on the National Register of Historic Places. The complete tour package—which includes the mansion, trophy room, car museum, airplanes, and touring bus—costs about $16. The phone number is 901-332-3322.

Every August, to commemorate the anniversary of Presley's passing, Elvis

International Tribute Week is held in Memphis. Hard-core fans come from all over the world to wade in Tennessee's liquid summer heat. The week's high point is a candlelight procession that starts along the wall by the street and moves up the drive and past the grave.

■ THE MEMPHIS MUSIC AND BLUES MUSEUM

97 South 2nd Street, Memphis

The city of Memphis is planning eventually to open a full-fledged music museum and memorabilia collection in the new Memphis Pyramid. Until then, the Memphis Music and Blues Museum, currently housed in a storefront near the Peabody Hotel downtown, offers a quick overview of Memphis' contributions to music history. The collection here comprises many old 78 records, special displays (W. C. Handy and "Rocket 88" are two subjects), quite a few nice photographs, and earphone stations where visitors can listen in on the real sounds of this most musical city.

The self-guided tour concludes with a display of photos of Elvis working out with his karate teacher.

The tour costs about $5, and the museum is open daily. The gift shop in front sells sacks of Sonny Boy Corn Meal, records, posters and, believe it or not, expensive vintage guitars. Call 901-525-4007.

■ SAM PHILLIPS RECORDING SERVICE

639 Madison Avenue, Memphis

Producer Sam Phillips opened the Sam Phillips Recording Service, his second Memphis studio, in about 1960 and began to chase his own legend. He was not to find another Elvis, but the studio has produced a few hits. The studio says that both "Wooly Bully" and "Little Red Riding Hood" by Sam the Sham and the Pharaohs were done here; likewise "I'm a Man" and "Train Kept A-Rollin'" by the Yardbirds. The Amazing Rhythm Aces worked out of this studio in the mid-Seventies and cut their hit "Third Rate Romance" here.

The Recording Service is still on Madison Avenue and remains a working studio.

4941 Summer Avenue, Memphis

It could be argued that chain hostelries are as much a part of rock 'n' roll as guitar strings, groupies, and hair mousse. It was at Summer Avenue in Memphis that the original Holiday Inn—home away from home for so many touring musicians—opened in August 1952.

Memphis entrepreneur Kemmons Wilson had come home from a family vacation disgusted with the quality of lodging he'd found on the road. Wilson raised funds for an inn, which he built near the intersection of two highways on Memphis' east side. The first unit had 120 rooms, and included such innovations as a bathroom, a telephone, and air conditioning in each room. Wilson put a swimming pool outside and announced that children could stay free. He made a fortune.

The site has another tie to rock legend: Sam Phillips, the Sun Records producer who discovered Elvis (and who sold the rights to Elvis' music for a pittance in the late Fifties), invested heavily in Holiday Inn. The investment made him wealthy, which is only fair, because Wilson was supposedly among the advisers who told Phillips that selling Presley to RCA was a good idea.

The building is no longer called Holiday Inn, and no mention is made on the premises of its legacy to the world. There's no reason to check in (although single rooms cost a mere $21.12), but do check it out. The phone number is 901-683-2411.

■ ROYAL RECORDING STUDIO

1320 South Lauderdale Street, Memphis

The building that eventually housed Royal Recording Studio opened in 1915 as the Shamrock Theater, a silent movie house. It later came to be known as the Rex, then the Royal. Soon after the Royal closed in 1955 a group of local entrepreneurs converted the space into the Royal Recording Studio and launched a new label, Hi Records. The studio's Fifties hits were rockabilly tunes and instrumentals such as "Smokey, Part 2" and "White Silver Sands" by Bill Black's Combo. Willie Mitchell, a local trumpeter and bandleader, began to direct Hi's recording output in 1963, and turned the company toward soul.

Mitchell cut a few minor hits in the Sixties, but didn't break through to the top of the charts until teaming with Al Green, in 1969. The sly funk of Mitchell's arrangements, combined with Green's straight-from-church vocals, made smashes of a string of Royal recordings, including "Can't Get Next to You," "Let's Stay Together," "Tired of Being Alone," and "Call Me." Mitchell had other successes in the Seventies, cutting records for Ann Peebles, George Jackson, and Bobby "Blue" Bland, but his work with Green is the reason to park in front of Royal and take pictures.

The studio still stands, near the corner of Richmond and Lauderdale streets, not far from the old Stax recording studios site. The word "Royal" is still faintly visible over the door and the place still functions as a recording studio. Although the official name has changed a few times over the years (to Hi Studios, then to Way-Low and, most recently, to Cream-Hi Records), local scenemakers still call it Royal.

Take Wellington Boulevard (called Danny Thomas Boulevard in town) south from Crump Boulevard or north from South Parkway. Turn east at Trigg Avenue, then south on Lauderdale Street.

■ **STAX STUDIOS**

---

926 East McLemore Avenue, Memphis

In 1960, Jim Stewart and Estelle Axton took over the vacant Capitol Theater at 926 East McLemore, which dated from 1931. Stewart, a banker and semiprofessional fiddler, had founded the country-oriented Satellite Records in a garage in 1957; Estelle, his sister, had mortgaged her house to pay for the company's first Ampex tape machine.

The duo tore out the seats of the old Capitol, set up a control room where the stage had been, hung sound-deadening drapes (home-sewn by Estelle) from the ceiling, and called it a studio. The lobby candy counter was converted to a record store.

The neighborhood was never a good one, but studio management had no qualms about enlisting local talent. Producer David Porter worked in the grocery store across the street. Booker T. Jones lived around the corner. Influenced by their neighbors' sensibilities, Stewart and Axton veered from country-western almost immediately.

Stax Studios—then . . .

. . . And now (Memphis)

Memphis disc jockey Rufus Thomas and his daughter Carla produced Satellite's first hit, "'Cause I Love You." Soon after, the studio signed a distribution deal with Atlantic and produced the Mar-Keys' "Last Night."

Later, they decided to change Satellite's name, and (St)ewart and (Ax)ton donated two letters each. What followed was "Green Onions," a second label called Volt, Sam and Dave, Otis Redding, Isaac Hayes, and hits, hits, hits.

The Stax sound was created by racially integrated groups of musicians working with material provided by house producers and performers. Atlantic Records fed talent (Sam and Dave, Wilson Pickett) to Stax, and Stax responded with songs and backing tracks. Key players at the studio included guitarist, songwriter, and producer Steve Cropper, bassists Lewis Steinberg and Duck Dunn, keyboardist Booker T. Jones, and drummer Al Jackson, Jr.

Also vital to Stax's success was the production and songwriting team of David Porter and Isaac Hayes, which turned out several classics. Once, during a Sam and Dave session at Stax in 1966, Porter slipped away to use the bathroom. When Hayes hounded him through the door to hurry back to the studio, Porter answered, "Hold on, man! I'm coming." And so a song was born.

A year later, in December 1967, Otis Redding and Steve Cropper recorded a song they'd written together, "(Sittin' on) The Dock of the Bay." Redding died in a plane crash in Wisconsin a few days after the session. Cropper had to return to the studio after Redding's death to finish the mix.

Financial disarray forced Stax to close in January 1976. The building stood empty for years, eventually became the property of the Southside Church of God in Christ, and then was demolished. The Stax address is a vacant lot now, denoted by a beat-up historical marker.

Some of the building's bricks and interior fixtures were supposedly preserved and placed in storage, in the hopes of recreating Stax's Studio A in one of several civic-improvement projects currently underway. The Memphis Pyramid, a modest structure at Front Street and Auction near downtown, is a possible home.

McLemore runs east-west between Highway 51 (Elvis Presley Boulevard) and Wellington (Danny Thomas Boulevard), four or five blocks north of South Parkway.

Booker T. and the MGs   "Green Onions"
"Hip Hug-Her"
"Time Is Tight"

Otis Redding   "These Arms of Mine"
"Mr. Pitiful"
"I've Been Loving You Too Long (to Stop Now)"
"Respect"
"I Can't Turn You Loose"
"Satisfaction"
"Fa-Fa-Fa-Fa-Fa (Sad Song)"
"Shake"
"(Sittin' on) The Dock of the Bay"

Rufus Thomas   "Walking the Dog"

Sam and Dave   "You Don't Know Like I Know"
"Hold On! I'm Comin' "
"When Something Is Wrong With My Baby"
"Soul Man"
"I Thank You"

Eddie Floyd   "Knock on Wood"
"Raise Your Hand"

Wilson Pickett   "In the Midnight Hour"
"634-5789 (Soulsville, U.S.A.)"
"Ninety-Nine and a Half (Won't Do)"

Albert King   "Born Under a Bad Sign"

Isaac Hayes   "(Theme From) Shaft"
Hot Buttered Soul

706 Union Avenue, Memphis

Would-be producer Sam Phillips quit a radio job in 1950 to found the Memphis Recording Service. His goal was to make quick money by selling personalized recordings of weddings and other social gatherings. Phillips also had a custom-recording sidelight, which in time would deliver a spectacular payoff.

In his spare time, Phillips devoted his creative energy to documenting the area's blues, gospel, rhythm and blues, country, and hillbilly music. Working out of an old radiator shop on Union Avenue, he was in the right place at the right time to help fuse all of that music into rock 'n' roll.

By 1950, Memphis had been an American music center for decades and teemed with great musicians. Phillips' first recordings, distributed through independent labels such as Duke, Chess, and RPM, were of the Beale Streeters (a group at times comprising B. B. King, Johnny Ace, Rosco Gordon, Bobby "Blue" Bland, and others), Howlin' Wolf, Joe Hill Louis, Rufus Thomas, and James Cotton. During this time, Phillips also established a relationship with Ike Turner, a young player and raconteur from Clarksdale, Mississippi. In 1951, Turner (who later acted as Phillips' talent scout in the South) brought his own combo up from the Delta. As mentioned earlier, "Rocket 88," issued under the name Jackie Brenston and His Delta Cats, was recorded with a busted amp and is considered by many—including Phillips—to be the first true rock 'n' roll record.

Dozens of songs claim that honor, but in truth there was no one first rock 'n' roll record. "Rocket 88"—a loud car song driven by fuzz-tone guitar—was certainly one of the coolest, and became a number one R & B hit. The next year, Phillips launched his own label, Sun Records.

Phillips' Memphis-blues period lasted from 1950 through mid-1954, by which time another Memphis music hybrid had captured his attention. In the summer of 1953, recent Humes High School graduate Elvis Presley came to Sun to cut a custom record. He paid the fee, $4 for two sides, and sang a couple of ballads, "My Happiness" and "That's When Your Heartaches Begin." Nothing resulted from the session.

Presley returned the following January and again paid to record. Someone at Sun (legend says it was Phillips' assistant, Marion Keisker) took notice. By

April 1954, Presley was a regular at the studio, and Phillips had teamed him with guitarist Scotty Moore and bass player Bill Black. That July the combo cut what has come to be considered a cultural Big Bang, "That's All Right," a jumping blues tune originally recorded by Arthur "Big Boy" Crudup.

Presley recorded a "B" side during the same session, an up-tempo romp through Bill Monroe's bluegrass standard, "Blue Moon of Kentucky." Within days, Dewey Phillips, host of the "Red, Hot, and Blue" Memphis radio show, was playing the record almost continuously. The song charted well locally, and Elvis, Scotty, and Bill began to play live. They also appeared on the "Grand Ole Opry" and "Louisiana Hayride" radio shows.

"Good Rockin' Tonight" followed in September 1954; then came "Mystery Train," "Baby, Let's Play House," and "Milkcow Blues Boogie." That's all it took. Elvis Presley was wildfire.

Sun's storefront recording setup witnessed many other classic performances. Jerry Lee Lewis made "Great Balls of Fire," "Whole Lot of Shakin' Goin On," and "Breathless" here; Billy Riley cut "Red Hot," and Carl Perkins recorded "Blue Suede Shoes." Roy Orbison's "Ooby Dooby" and Johnny Cash's "Folsom Prison Blues," "I Walk the Line," "Home of the Blues," and "Cry! Cry! Cry!" are other Sun creations.

A legendary Sun session took place in December 1956, when Presley, who had left Sun for RCA a year earlier, dropped by the studio with a lady friend from Las Vegas. Presley, Lewis, and Perkins gathered around a piano to sing some gospel tunes. Phillips started the tape machine, then called Johnny Cash, at the time Phillips' newest protege. Cash came down and posed for pictures with the others, but didn't join them in the music. The once-in-a-lifetime gathering came to be known as the Million Dollar Quartet.

Sam Phillips moved his recording operation out of the Sun building a few years after breaking with Elvis and set up another studio called Sam Phillips Recording Service. The old Sun Studio was restored and opened as a tourist attraction in the Eighties, and the original front office now serves as a gift shop and staging area for tours.

The studio itself, a tiny room with a baffled ceiling and walls blanketed by acoustic tiles, is usually set up as if a session were underway—a vintage guitar or two, an old microphone, and a drum set are realistically posed, although none of those particular instruments was actually used at Sun. A control panel

Sun Studio (Memphis)

stands against the back wall. The studio is also decorated with photos from Sun's golden age.

Tour guides point out that Sun is still a working studio. Ringo Starr, U2, and Michelle Shocked, among others, have recorded here in recent years, and a segment of U2's concert movie *Rattle and Hum* was filmed at Sun. The complex also includes a restaurant next door, as well as an upstairs record store that specializes in Memphis-made music.

Call 901-521-0664 for more information. The studio is open every day except Thanksgiving, Christmas, and New Year's Day. Informal tours ($4.50) are conducted from 10 A.M. to 6 P.M. Keep in mind that the place is small and little of what you see inside is authentic. There's not much to do except go to the middle of the room and look at the walls. For most visitors, glad just to stand where the Million Dollar Quartet stood, that's plenty.

■ WILSON WORLD HOTEL

3677 Elvis Presley Boulevard, Memphis

Wilson World, the latest venture of Holiday Inn founder Kemmons Wilson, is a chain of comfortable pink boxes. The Memphis outlet is right across the street from Graceland, and free Elvis Presley movies are shown on one of the hotel's TV channels round the clock. This is the perfect place to stay if you plan a total Elvis experience in Memphis: in addition to the Elvis Channel, there are the huge portraits of Elvis in the lobby and Elvis music, broadcast throughout the Graceland tour staging area, is clearly audible from the Wilson World parking lot. And your tour van awaits—only a few hundred yards from the hotel lobby. If you can tear yourself away from the King, one of the other Wilson World television channels broadcasts nonstop interviews and positive profiles of your host, Kemmons Wilson.

Rates are very reasonable. Call 901-332-1000 for reservations.

Nashville

■ BRADLEY'S STUDIO/CBS

34 Music Square East, Nashville

In the Fifties, producer Owen Bradley built studios in Nashville with the goal of making country records. Bradley's Quonset Hut (as the big studio came to be known) and the adjoining smaller studio produced classic country in abundance during its run, including all of Patsy Cline's hits. The larger room was also used as a television production studio.

Many of the site's biggest rock 'n' roll moments came in 1956. Gene Vincent and the Bluecaps made "Be-Bop-A-Lula" and "Woman Love" in that year. The studio's recording engineers were a little thrown by the rock combo's sound levels during "Be-Bop-A-Lula," so Vincent actually recorded the vocal track standing in the hallway between the hut and the smaller studio. Johnny Burnette and the Rock 'n' Roll Trio came here to cut "Tear It Up" and "Train Kept A-Rollin'." Paul Burlison's guitar tone on "Train" is still the industry standard for gritty licks. Also in '56, Decca Records sent Buddy Holly to Bradley to record some country-style songs. Those sessions didn't work out well, and Holly's big successes came later, at Norman Petty's studio in Clovis, New Mexico.

Bradley sold the studio in the Sixties. Columbia took over, and built offices and recording space up and around the original structures. Bob Dylan came here to cut parts of several albums, including *Blonde on Blonde, John Wesley Harding, Nashville Skyline*, and *Self Portrait*. During the late Sixties, the Byrds recorded some of *Sweetheart of the Rodeo* here.

Columbia eventually closed down the studio, and the completely re-modeled building now only houses business offices.

4 Music Square East, Nashville

I f rock 'n' roll's hall of fame is as beautifully done as country music's, all will be right with the world. The museum area tells the whole story of the country sound, from Vernon Dalhart through Randy Travis, and the actual Hall of Fame wing is exquisite. Some rock 'n' roll-related highlights:

- Performance costumes, old instruments, and vehicles of the stars are all on view. The costumes include a lime green his-and-hers combo once worn by Dolly Parton and Porter Wagoner. One of the old guitars belonged to Gram Parsons; another is an early Les Paul electric fashioned out of a four-by-four plank.

- The star of the star vehicles, of course, is Elvis Presley's so-called Solid Gold Cadillac (it's actually painted white), a gift to Elvis from RCA. The car's top flips up so visitors can see its glistening interior, and as the top rises, a recorded voice says, "Many country artists have displayed affection for the material symbols of their success. . ." Inside the car there's a built-in shoe polisher, refrigerator (with ice trays), fully equipped personal-grooming kit, on-board television set, telephone, and record player.

- A section of the hall has a collection of original lyric scribblings and chord sheets. One fascinating display attempts to explain the cryptic notation system used by Nashville studio musicians.

- The Artist Gallery is a changing exhibit devoted to the life and times of a chosen performer. Past featured artists have included Dolly Parton and Johnny Cash.

- Nearby is the RCA Studio B Museum, a tour of which is included with admission to the Hall. It's the actual studio used by RCA-Nashville during the Fifties, Sixties, and Seventies. The museum today is a multimedia extravaganza and offers the most technically informative studio tour anywhere. Elvis Presley recorded in this studio, as did Roy Orbison and the Everly Brothers.

The Hall of Fame is typically open 9 A.M. to 5 P.M. every day (longer hours in the summer) and admission is $6.50. Don't miss the gift shop. The phone number is 615-255-5333.

1525 McGavock Street, Nashville

1525 McGavock Street, once the property of the Methodist Television, Radio and Film Commission, was RCA's Nashville recording base when Elvis Presley signed with the label. He came here from Memphis on January 10, 1956, and cut several singles, including "Heartbreak Hotel," "I Got a Woman," "Money Honey," and "I Was the One." The Everly Brothers' "Bye Bye Love" was also recorded here during that era. The studio is now occupied by the Jim Owens Companies, which produce programming for the Nashville Network. Call 615-256-7700 for more information.

■ RYMAN AUDITORIUM

116 Fifth Avenue North, Nashville

The Ryman Auditorium was built as a tabernacle in 1892 by riverboat baron Thomas G. Ryman. The legend is that Ryman, who ran boats for gamblers and other hell-bound sorts, saw Samuel R. Jones preaching in a tent and vowed to erect a cathedral for him.

The resulting structure ended up as a cathedral to yodeling hillbillies and twanging guitars: the Grand Ole Opry moved into the Ryman in 1943, and its show was broadcast weekly via radio from this stage for 31 years. In 1974, the pageant moved to Opryland, an amusement park on the edge of town.

The original Grand Ole Opry had a powerful influence on American popular music. Each week the people who invented rock 'n' roll kept one ear glued to the radio broadcast from the Ryman.

Today, a self-guided tour through the musty backstage area tells most of the story. One episode, though, is not highlighted. In 1954, a young singer named Elvis Presley came to the Opry to perform but was treated poorly by the staff. In fact, after his rendition of "That's All Right" and "Blue Moon of Kentucky," Opry manager Jim Denny advised Elvis to go back to driving trucks.

The Ryman is open from 8:30 A.M. to 4:30 P.M. every day. T tour costs $2.50. Call 615-254-1445 for more information.

THE MIDWEST

ILLINOIS

Champaign

■ **FIRST FARM AID SITE**

Memorial Stadium, University of Illinois, Champaign

The first of the Farm Aid concerts was held at Memorial Stadium on September 22, 1985. Organized by Willie Nelson and John Cougar Mellencamp, the benefit publicized the plight of American farmers. It rained.

Chicago

■ **BUCKINGHAM FOUNTAIN**

Between Michigan Avenue and Lake Shore Drive, Chicago

Chicago produced several briefly successful pop bands in the late Sixties and early Seventies—the Buckinghams ("Don't You Care," "Kind of a Drag," "Mercy, Mercy, Mercy," and "Hey Baby They're Playing Our Song"), Shadows of Knight (a quickie cover of Them's "Gloria"), and the Ides of March ("Vehicle") were among them. (During this same era, Chicago also produced Chicago, a band that was successful quite a bit longer.) The Buckingham Fountain supposedly gave the Buckinghams their name, and it stands today as a testament to the Chicago club bands who got lucky.

■ **CHESS RECORDS**

2120 South Michigan Avenue, Chicago

2120 South Michigan Avenue is one of the great addresses in all of rock 'n' roll history. For ten years this building was headquarters and recording base for Chess Records, the independent label most responsible for the dissemination of electrified Delta blues during the Forties and Fifties and, later, the epochal sounds of Chuck Berry and Bo Diddley. The earlier music—of Muddy Waters, Willie Dixon, Howlin' Wolf, Sonny Boy Williamson, and Little Walter—was called Chicago blues. The later, by Chuck, Bo, and others, was rock 'n' roll.

By World War II, Chicago was already a blues center, and was becoming more so with every run of the Illinois Central up from Mississippi. Leonard and Phil Chess, Polish-Jewish immigrants to America in the late Twenties, ran black nightclubs on Chicago's South Side, and from there the jump to sound studios was a natural. They founded Aristocrat Records in 1947 and began recording the players they hired for their clubs. Aristocrat releases included dance-band tunes and even a few polkas, but the focus from the start was jazz and blues.

Aristocrat changed its name to Chess in 1950 and over the next decade specialized in the hard, electric sound of Chicago blues. The company also distributed some of the jazz records made by producer Sam Phillips' Sun Studios down in Memphis.

In 1955, Chess (and its offshoot label, Checker) already was the hottest record company going. It got hotter still when Bo Diddley and Chuck Berry signed on. Diddley's contribution to rock 'n' roll was the relentless hambone beat. Berry wrote the book on baseline rock guitar.

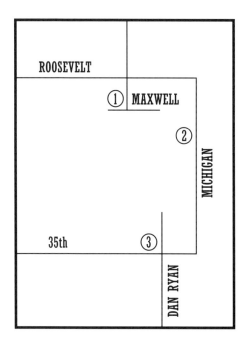

Three selected sites around Chicago:
1) Maxwell Street
2) Chess Records
3) The Comiskey Park burial ground

All this time, Chess had been operating out of various rented storefront offices around the South Side, but in 1957 the company moved to the two-story building at 2120 South Michigan. Buddy Guy, Etta James, and Koko Taylor worked on records here, and Bo Diddley cut the 1959 hit "Say Man." Chuck Berry recorded many songs on South Michigan, including "Rock 'n' Roll Music" and, on February 29, 1958, "Johnny B. Goode."

When British blues bands invaded America in the next decade, they homed in on Chess. The Yardbirds and the Rolling Stones (that group's very name was an homage to the Chess sound, and especially to the great Muddy Waters) both recorded here.

Keith Richards claims that the Stones arrived on their first visit to the studio to find Muddy Waters painting the ceiling. (This story has another permutation: the arriving visitor is a record-company executive, who shows up at one of the Chess brothers' houses to find Muddy painting there. The keepers of Chicago blues lore discount these tales.) While at the studio the Stones cut an instrumental and named it after the Chess street address; one of their later visits to Chess resulted in preliminary tracks for "Satisfaction."

The Chess building is situated in the heart of what was known as Chicago's Record Row. Among the labels headquartered nearby was Vee Jay, remembered now as home to such artists as the Dells, the Spaniels, the El Dorados, John Lee Hooker, Jimmy Reed, Dee Clark, Gene Chandler, and the Four Seasons. Vee Jay—a rare black-owned independent run by husband and wife Vivian (Vee) Carter and Jimmy (Jay) Bracken—is also remembered as the first company to release Beatles music in America. In early 1963, Capitol owned the distribution rights to all the Beatles material, which was selling by the millions in England, but passed on it. Vee Jay latched on for "Please Please Me," "From Me to You" and, later that year, an album titled *Introducing the Beatles*. None of the records sold well at first, but Capitol, finally sensing the group's potential, began slapping Vee Jay with cease-and-desist lawsuits. Not much later, the little label folded.

Chess moved out of 2120 South Michigan in 1967; Leonard Chess died two years later. By the early Seventies, both Phil and Marshall Chess (Leonard's son, who had joined the company in the late Sixties) had left the music business. The upstairs part of the 2120 building was occupied through the Seventies by a school for theater and dance; then, in 1980, the Chess family sold the building to Gerald Sims, a former Chess session musician. The studio was granted landmark status by the city of Chicago in 1990, but so far has not been opened to the public.

Parts of the interior remain as they were in 1960; other elements—the building is still a working studio—have been updated. The basement and the first floor—used for dreary office space in the old days—are now mostly empty. The main studio upstairs looks like all recording studios: brown fabric on the walls, mood lighting, a few musicians fiddling with equipment. There's no memorabilia, no collection of old posters. But the transition to museum, should it ever come, will be easy. Just let the people walk up the stairs, put them in the studio and tell them "Johnny B. Goode" was made here.

■ THE PLAYBOY MANSION

1336–1340 North State Parkway

The Playboy Mansion was Hugh Hefner's home until he moved to Los Angeles. After that, the building (as Hefner Hall) housed thirty-five first-year students of the Art Institute of Chicago. The institute put the mansion up for sale in the late Eighties.

■ COMISKEY PARK BURIAL SITE

324 West 35th Street, Chicago

The old Comiskey ball park witnessed concerts, prize fights, gambling scandals, riots—even baseball games—during its life. The Beatles, for example, played Comiskey on one of their American tours.

The grand ball yard's most infamous rock 'n' roll moment came on July 12, 1979, when White Sox owner and promoter nonpareil Bill Veeck filled the place with grimy, disco-hating, South Side longhairs. The event was called Disco Demolition Night, and everyone who showed up carrying a disco record got in to that evening's double-header between the Detroit Tigers and the Chicago White Sox for 98 cents. Between games, the records were tossed in a bin on the field and blown up. A riot ensued—tens of thousands of records were skimmed over the field like frisbees, accompanied by turf tearing and head banging—and forced the cancellation of the second half of the bill. The disco demolishers actually had control of the field for about an hour that night, before the Chicago police moved in and settled things.

The old Comiskey is history, replaced in 1990 by a new park right next door.

■ DEMON DOGS

944 West Fullerton Avenue, Chicago

Demon Dogs proprietor Peter Schivarelli befriended members of the group Chicago during their days at De Paul University across the street. Still affiliated with the group's management team, Schivarelli now also peddles terrific hot dogs and fries on the side. Demon Dogs is located directly below some atmospheric "El" tracks and must be the only shrine in existence to the band that made "Color My World" a prom staple. On these walls, Chicago gold records, tour regalia, and autographed photos compete for space alongside Vienna Beef posters. A Zildjian cymbal signed by former group drummer Danny Seraphine is displayed opposite the order counter; a saxophone once played by the band's Walt Parazaider is posted near the cash register.

Diners at Demon Dogs chew to the accompaniment of nonstop hits by—any guesses? Schivarelli apparently is also making Demon Dogs a must-see for touring musicians, in addition to the ever-changing assembly of players who still call themselves Chicago (the original members moved from the city before making it big and rarely return except to play concerts). Judging from the walls, Demon Dogs has welcomed such luminaries as Eddie Van Halen, Poison, Jimmy Buffet, and a couple of Playboy Playmates.

Fullerton is a major east-west route through the north side of town, and Demon Dogs (phone-in orders: 312-281-2001) is reachable via car, bus, and elevated train.

■ THE EARL OF OLD TOWN

1615 North Wells, Chicago

The Earl, the nexus of the Chicago folk scene in the late Sixties and early Seventies, produced Steve Goodman ("City of New Orleans") and John Prine ("Hello In There"), among others. Now it's a bar called the Last Act Company, where the phone number is 312-440-4915.

63 West Ontario Street, Chicago

In addition to the usual gold and platinum records from around the rock world, this Hard Rock Cafe houses items affiliated with Chicago-area musicians. The pieces here are not likely to wander to other stores in the chain. For example, there's some Willie Dixon stuff on display in the balcony, and a platinum single awarded to Survivor (a band made up mostly of local musicians) for "Eye of the Tiger" is up on the south side of the main floor. Bobby Lamm's electric piano, used for early recordings by Chicago, and a guitar discarded by Cheap Trick's Rick Nielsen are nearby. Also worth looking for is one of George Harrison's jackets (worn on the 1964 Beatles tour of America) hung on the building's north wall.

A strange McDonald's, filled with things relating to rock 'n' roll (including a statue of the Beatles) is just across the street to the west of the Hard Rock. Also nearby is the downtown Chicago branch of Ed Debevic's, a Fifties-theme restaurant popular with people who like loud meals.

The Hard Rock Cafe's phone number is 312-943-2252.

■ LUDWIG DRUMS

1728 North Damen Street, Chicago

For fifty years, North Damen Street was the manufacturing headquarters for Ludwig Drums—Ringo Starr's and Hal Blaine's Ludwig sets were made here. The company left the area in 1985 and now operates out of North Carolina. The Chicago site was remodeled into condominiums.

Slingerland drums were also manufactured in Chicago, at nearby 1325 Belden Street, until the company moved to suburban Niles in the mid-Sixties.

The South Side

For most of the twentieth century, Chicago's South Side was the place blues purveyors came. There were clubs here, record companies, and a giant audience fed by heavy-industry jobs. Remnants of those times remain, here and there, and it's possible to see the choicest sites in a single afternoon. Here's the itinerary:

■ 43RD STREET

It's not marked very well, but 43rd Street is more or less known as Muddy Waters Drive. His longtime headquarters in town was Pepper's Lounge, at 503 East 43rd. Another well-known blues house along this way is the New Checkerboard Lounge, at 423 East 43rd. The Checkerboard gained its fame because touring Rolling Stones would sometimes come here to jam with blues musicians. Now the place is popular with tourists. The phone number is 312-624-3240.

■ MAXWELL STREET

To get to Maxwell Street, drive west on Roosevelt to Halstead, then head south for three blocks. You will notice that this is not the South Side at all, but the West Side. Nonetheless, it's a legendary blues spot. Maxwell Street, now home to a few odd swap-meet street stalls, once was a major center of black life in Chicago; the shopping strip went on for blocks and live music filled the air. The scene is much reduced these days, although it's still possible to get a wonderful Polish sausage here. Nate's Delicatessen, at 807 West Maxwell, was the setting for Aretha Franklin's big scene in *The Blues Brothers*. When nearby Chess Records released Muddy Waters' first single, Waters came to Maxwell Street to buy some copies for himself.

■ THE REGAL THEATER
47th Street and Martin Luther King Jr. Drive

The Regal Theater was a palace in its day, the top black entertainment venue in the Midwest. The Jackson 5 opened for the Temptations here; B. B. King recorded *Live at the Regal*. Stevie Wonder's manic hit "Fingertips—Pt. 2" was taped during a Motown Revue show here in 1962.

The Regal site is at the southeast corner of 47th Street and Martin Luther King Jr. Drive. It's now a parking garage.

■ THE 708 CLUB
708 East 47th Street

The 708 Club was one of the leading blues joints in town in the Fifties and Sixties. Otis Rush and the young Bo Diddley cut their teeth on this stage. Unfortunately, it's closed now.

East St. Louis

■ THE COSMOPOLITAN CLUB

17th Street and Bond Avenue, East St. Louis

Struggling local guitarist Chuck Berry joined Sir John's Trio for a New Year's Eve show at the Cosmopolitan in 1953, after which piano wonder Johnnie Johnson (the Sir part of the combo) asked Berry to join the band. So the club is considered pivotal to the Chuck Berry story, and some atmospheric footage of the interior was included in the film *Hail, Hail Rock 'n' Roll*.

The Cosmopolitan has been in and out of business, so there's no telling what it will look like when you show up.

Edwardsville

■ HOLIDAY INN

Interstate 270 and Route 157, Edwardsville

The acoustics of the Edwardsville Holiday Inn have been preserved for posterity: Jackson Browne recorded a few cuts for his live album *Running on Empty*—"Cocaine" and "Shaky Town" were recorded in Room 124 here—during a tour layover in Edwardsville. *Running on Empty* was unique not only because it was the first successful live album comprising unreleased material, but also because of the oddball places Browne chose to record some of the songs. The hits ("Running on Empty" and the "Load-Out"/"Stay" medley) were taped inarenas, but other songs came to be in backstage rehearsal areas, hotel rooms, and even on a moving bus "somewhere in New Jersey."

The Holiday Inn is now called the Knight's Inn, and a night in Room 124 costs about $40. Call 618-656-3000 for reservations.

INDIANA

Fairmount

■ **JAMES DEAN'S GRAVE**

Park Cemetery, County Road 150E

Fairmount was Dean's hometown, and it's where you can find him today. A couple of local museums (the Fairmount Historical Museum, 203 East Washington; the James Dean Gallery, 425 North Main Street) handle cultists who arrive, looking for Dean's roots. In the late Eighties, former Smiths lead singer (and Dean biographer) Morrissey filmed a video for the song "Suedehead" at Dean's grave site.

Freetown

Freetown is a small hamlet about an hour straight south of Indianapolis. In his salad days John Mellencamp worked at the local Indiana Bell plant, and once accidentally disconnected all phone service to Freetown. The episode prompted him to consider the damage he could do with a large public-address system, and, eventually, a career change.

Since then, despite worldwide stardom, Mellencamp has maintained a residence in Seymour, Indiana, about twelve miles east of Freetown. He also spends time in Bloomington, a college town nearby.

Freetown is on Highway 58, off Interstate 65.

Gary

■ THE JACKSON FAMILY HOME

2400 Jackson Street, Gary

The world's oddest performing family was raised at 2400 Jackson Street in Gary. "Jackson," by the way, is the street's original name—not a tribute to any of the singing Jacksons.

The street runs through town just north of the Frank Borman Expressway.

Indianapolis

■ MARKET SQUARE ARENA

300 East Market Street, Indianapolis

Elvis Presley handed down his last sweaty scarf from the stage of the Market Square Arena, on June 26, 1977. Although the Arena's main function is basketball, the ticket lobby on the sixth floor has a small display of last-concert memorabilia, and a local Elvis fan club holds a memorial service every year on the show's anniversary.

The arena's number is 317-639-6411.

IOWA

Clear Lake City

■ BUDDY HOLLY CRASH SITE

Off State Road 20, north of Clear Lake

On the day the music died, Clear Lake City is where it happened. The quiet cornfield here may be the saddest place in rock 'n' roll history.

At about 1 A.M. on February 3, 1959, a single-engine Beechcraft Bonanza

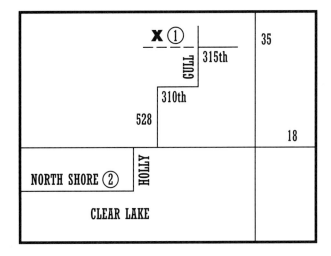

Buddy Holly crash site
& other significant sites
near Clear Lake:
1) The crash memorial
2) The Surf Ballroom

left the nearby Mason City airport, bound for Fargo, North Dakota. Light snow was falling, the wind was gusting to 35 miles per hour, it was 18 degrees. Buddy Holly, Ritchie Valens, J. P. "Big Bopper" Richardson, and local pilot Roger Peterson were onboard. The plane took off to the south and then turned back to the north. It crashed in a cornfield about eight miles from the airport, killing everyone. The wreckage wasn't discovered until about 9:30 the next morning.

For years afterward, the event had an almost mystical impact. (Don McLean's "American Pie" is only one example.) When the Beatles first came to America in February 1964, they were scheduled to fly from New York to Washington, D.C., for a concert following their appearance on "The Ed Sullivan Show." But a snowstorm came up and the group remembered Buddy. They insisted on traveling by train.

Holly's plane hit ground in the middle of the field and skidded about 500 feet. A metal marker has been placed where the wreckage was found. Getting to the spot is tricky. Step-by-step, here's the route:

1) Interstate 35 is the main road to Clear Lake.
2) From I-35, take Highway 18 west into town.
3) Turn onto a road labeled S28 going north from Highway 18. There's a gas station on the northeast corner of the intersection.
4) Drive five and a half miles on S28, then turn right onto 310th Street. Turn left immediately onto Gull Avenue, a gravel road.
5) Drive north on Gull for a half-mile, stopping at 315th Street. Park.

Where the Music Died—February 3, 1959 (Clear Lake, Iowa)

6) Walk west past the sign marking 315th Street, into the cornfield there. Keep walking west, on the north side of the wire fence, for half a mile. Four young oak trees (planted by the farmer who owns this land to represent the four victims of the crash) mark the memorial, which is sunk in cement against the fence.

According to Clear Lake sources, the landowner allows people to walk to the marker, as long as they mind their manners. And the corn.

■ THE SURF BALLROOM

460 North Shore Drive, Clear Lake City

Buddy Holly, Ritchie Valens, and the Big Bopper came to Iowa as part of the Winter Dance Party tour. It was a package deal, and included Dion and the Belmonts and Frankie Sardo. The group traveled the upper Midwest by bus, starting in Milwaukee and going through Duluth and Green Bay to the Surf Ballroom in Clear Lake.

Traveling conditions were awful; the buses were junkers. The day before the party played Clear Lake, one bus broke down completely outside Green Bay and the passengers had to burn newspapers in the aisles to keep warm. Carl Bunch, Buddy Holly's drummer, got frostbite anyway.

By the time the group reached Clear Lake, Holly had decided to fly the next leg of the trip. He was tired, of course, but he was also concerned about his band's appearance: there hadn't been any time during the previous few tour stops to launder the group's stage outfits. Holly—*he wanted to fly ahead to do laundry!*—chartered a four-seater plane for himself and band members Waylon Jennings and Tommy Allsup.

Admission to the concert that night was $1.25. About 1,500 showed up for the show, which by all accounts was fabulous. Valens had one of the hottest singles in the country at the time, "Donna," with "La Bamba" on the flip side. The Bopper's "Chantilly Lace" had been a chart hit for six months. Sometime during the evening, Richardson talked Jennings out of his seat on the plane. Valens won Allsup's spot in a coin toss. The three stars left the Surf for the airport at about midnight.

The Surf today is a time machine unlike anything else—step through the front door and you're in the Forties. The place is typical of the kind of ballroom that went up all over this part of the country during the big-band days. The main room was built in 1948 and has a tall, domed roof and a maple dance floor. A seating area, with tables, booths, and a couple of bars, runs around the perimeter of the room, and there's a little cafe attached on one side. Cloud machines project floating nimbus puffs against the black sky of the ceiling and one wall has murals that are changed to reflect the season. Much of the other wall space is devoted to old photos and newspaper stories. Even the phone booths in the Surf's lobby are historic. Surf managers Bruce and Sue Christensen located and reinstalled the phone where Ritchie Valens and Buddy Holly made their last calls—Buddy's was to his wife Maria, at home in New York City.

A stone memorializing the Winter Dance Party bill (plus pilot Peterson) stands in the front yard. The Surf has applied for placement on the National Register of Historic Places and is officially designated a museum, but it still remains a lively music venue. In the years since Buddy Holly's finale, the Yardbirds, Roy Orbison, Joan Jett, the Everly Brothers, Bobby Darin, Tommy James, Mitch Ryder, the Turtles, Sam the Sham, and Jerry Lee Lewis have played the stage. There's live music of some kind almost every weekend. The main event on the Surf's calendar is the annual Buddy Holly Tribute, held on the first weekend in February. Oldies bands are booked and Holly fans converge from all over the world.

The Surf is located in downtown Clear Lake, just south of Highway 18, the access road off Interstate 35. Turn south from 18 onto Buddy Holly Place, the third stoplight after you exit the interstate, then make a right onto North Shore. Call 515-357-6151 for more information.

MICHIGAN

Detroit

■ COBO ARENA
---

600 Civic Center Drive, Detroit

Bob Seger recorded his *Live Bullet* album at the Cobo Arena in September 1975. Seger has played this hall more than twenty times over the years. J. Geils and Journey have both taped live records here, too.

The number at Cobo, where some concerts are still occasionally held, is 313-567-6000.

■ *CREEM* MAGAZINE OFFICES

3729 Cass Avenue, Detroit

A national rock magazine based in Michigan? In the good old days—as the Sixties turned into the Seventies, back when Dave Marsh was editor—it worked. The original *Creem* (which is now a New York glossy under different ownership) operated out of the second floor of 3729 Cass Avenue.

■ THE FLAME SHOW BAR

4664 John R Street, Detroit

The headliner at the Flame Show Bar was Sam Cooke. The bar opened in April 1950, and young Berry Gordy came here in his scuffling days to pitch songs—one of his customers was Jackie Wilson. (For a time, Gordy's sisters ran the photography and cigarette concession.) The Flame's house band was Maurice King and the Wolverines; later, King would become one of the key music directors at Gordy's Motown.

The Flame has been extinguished.

■ THE FOX THEATER

2211 Woodward Avenue, Detroit

The Fox Theater, a downtown movie-and-vaudeville palace, was built in 1928. Motown Revue shows appeared here often—Christmas was a traditional Motown-at-the-Fox date every year—and the venue remains a fine example of theater rehabilitation, with a full schedule of touring shows and concerts.

It's restored. It's beautiful. Call 313-567-6000.

■ THE GRANDE BALLROOM

8952 Grand River Road, Detroit

The Grande (pronounced "Grandee") is fondly if dimly remembered by locals as their own psychedelic ballroom. It's also significant as the 1968 recording site for the incendiary MC5 debut manifesto, *Kick Out the Jams*.

■ MOTOWN MUSEUM

2648 West Grand Boulevard, Detroit

Berry Gordy, Jr., a would-be record producer, bought a little bungalow at 2648 West Grand Boulevard in 1959. A few years later he owned almost the whole block. Gordy named Motown's corporate headquarters here Hitsville U.S.A., and it wasn't mere brag. Consider:

"Ain't No Mountain High
 Enough"
"Ain't Nothing Like the Real
 Thing"
"Ain't Too Proud to Beg"
"Baby, I Need Your Loving"
"Baby Love"
"Can I Get a Witness"
"Dancing in the Street"

"For Once in My Life"
"Get Ready"
"Going to a Go-Go"
"Heat Wave"
"Hitch Hike"
"How Sweet It Is (to Be Loved By
 You)"
"I Can't Help Myself"
"I Hear a Symphony"

"I Heard It Through the
   Grapevine"
"(I Know) I'm Losing You"
"Inner City Blues"
"I Second That Emotion"
"It Takes Two"
"Mercy Mercy Me (the Ecology)"
"My Guy"
"My Girl"
"Nowhere to Run"
"Ooo Baby Baby"
"Please Mr. Postman"
"Reach Out I'll Be There"
"Shop Around"
"Shotgun"

"Someday We'll Be Together"
"Standing in the Shadows of
   Love"
"Stop! In the Name of Love"
"The Tracks of My Tears"
"The Way You Do the Things You
   Do"
"What Does It Take (to Win Your
   Love)"
"What's Going On"
"Where Did Our Love Go"
"You Can't Hurry Love"
"You're All I Need to Get By"
"You've Really Got a Hold on
   Me"

And that's the short list.

Gordy had been a worker in a Detroit auto plant, and he took an assembly-line approach to hit making. Every department worked independently. Staff songwriters and producers created the tunes and wrote the arrangements, the house band laid down the tracks. When the marquee names weren't in the studio cutting songs or touring, they were in one of the buildings down the street getting etiquette lessons or learning new dance steps. Gordy hired a house choreographer, Cholly Atkins, and set up a "finishing school" for performers. Maxine Powell was the director, and coached Motown acts on offstage deportment. Maurice King was music coordinator and the main vocal instructor. Gordy himself led regular quality-control meetings, as if the company product were sedans instead of songs. And it worked, for one glorious decade.

Motown's key writers and producers were Brian Holland, Eddie Holland, Lamont Dozier, Harvey Fuqua, Johnny Bristol, Nick Ashford, Valerie Simpson, Norman Whitfield, and Smokey Robinson. And, of course, Gordy himself.

The mostly anonymous killer Motown rhythm section—their in-house tag was the Funk Brothers—were Earl Van Dyke (piano and band leader), Benny "Papa Zita" Benjamin (drummer), and James Jamerson (first genius of the Fender Precision Bass). In the early days, the band was paid by the session—$5, $7, or $10 per single. They were later put on salary, and Gordy tried to discourage the group from moonlighting, but they did sneak out for a couple of notable wildcat sessions: Edwinn Starr's "Agent Double-O Soul," recorded elsewhere in Detroit, and Jackie Wilson's "(Your Love Keeps Lifting Me) Higher and Higher," cut in Chicago.

The studio itself, a large add-on room at the back of the bungalow, was nicknamed "The Snake Pit" by those who staffed it. Part of the secret behind the massive beat on "Dancing in the Street" is the sound of tire chains hitting the studio's floor. And those handclaps in "Baby Love"? Smacking two-by-fours.

One night in 1961, Gordy was having a steak dinner in his upstairs office when producers Brian Holland and Ronnie White burst in to show him their latest discovery: eleven-year-old Steveland Morris, who played piano, harmonica, and bongos for the boss that evening and soon had himself a record contract as Little Stevie Wonder.

Marvin Gaye was another multi-talented Motown performer. He was famous for writing and singing, but behind the scenes he played drums (on "Please Mr. Postman" by the Marvelettes) and keyboards (on Martha and the Vandellas' "Dancing in the Street").

In 1967, Gordy moved Motown's business offices from the Grand Avenue buildings to an office tower on Woodward Avenue in Detroit. The studio remained in use until the whole company moved to the West Coast in the early Seventies. Some offices stayed at Hitsville in the Seventies and Eighties, but the Detroit site's main role appears to have been as a place to stockpile Berry Gordy memorabilia. The Hitsville U.S.A. studios opened to the public as a museum in 1985.

The Motown Museum tour today is fabulous, of course. It starts with a little video presentation, then a guide takes you back to the old control room and studio. Except for some promotional cutouts of Lionel Richie-esque performers, the Snake Pit looks just as it did in 1967: the music stands have charts, microphone cords hang from the ceiling, there are drums in the drum booth and a set of vibes (the subliminal secret of the Motown sound) near the door. The toy piano used to make bell sounds on Supremes records is in a glass case. The candy machine in the control room is stocked.

The tour proceeds to upstairs offices, which now display gold records and old publicity photos. Michael Jackson has his own little space here (don't miss the flower-power bellbottoms Michael wore as one of the Jackson 5), as do most of the Motown stars. Last stop on the tour is the gift shop.

Throughout, the archival presentation is not always well-preserved. In some cases, old album jackets are just pinned to the wall.

Museum operators are planning considerable expansion and renovation for the buildings. A glass atrium/entry area may someday be added between the two main bungalows, and the video-presentation space will be expanded.

The old studio will not be touched, however. As it is now, visitors squint at the same crummy fluorescent light fixtures that once caused Smokey Robinson and James Jamerson to squint. And that's the whole point.

Admission is $3 for adults. Hours are 10 A.M. to 5 P.M., Monday through Saturday; 2 P.M. to 5 P.M. on Sunday. The phone number is 313-875-2264.

■ NEW BETHEL BAPTIST CHURCH

8450 C. L. Franklin Boulevard, Detroit

The Reverend C. L. Franklin presided at the New Bethel Baptist Church in the Fifties, and in addition to being a pastor he was a recording artist with Chess Records in Chicago. His three daughters regularly sang at church services. Sisters Carolyn and Erma Franklin you may not recall. Sister Aretha you do.

The church doesn't exploit its role in the history of soul, pop, and rock—gospel is the music that matters here. Services are at 8 A.M., 10:45 A.M., and 9 P.M. every Sunday, and the nighttime service is broadcast live on Detroit radio. To get here, take the C. L. Franklin Boulevard exit off of Interstate 94. The phone number is 313-894-5788.

■ THE ROOSTERTAIL

100 Marquette Drive, Detroit

The two-story Roostertail was once home to the weekly Motown Mondays showcase performances. Now it's used for special occasions, typically big corporate shows, conventions, and receptions. Sometimes old Motown acts are hired to perform for the private parties.

The place doesn't advertise and isn't generally open to the public. The phone number is 313-822-1234.

■ THE TWENTY GRAND

1520 14th Street, Detroit

The Twenty Grand, along with the Flame Show Bar, was a favorite after-work spot for the Motown employees. The Four Tops were sitting in the audience at the Twenty Grand in 1964 when Brian Holland approached and told them he'd just written a hit for them called "Baby, I Need Your Loving." The party went back to Hitsville after the show and cut it that very night.

Another night, in 1966, the Supremes were rehearsing at the Twenty Grand, and many of the Motown top brass were in the audience. After Florence Ballard had sung the first few bars of "People," her great solo number, Berry Gordy walked onstage, told her to stop, and gave the song to Diana Ross. Gordy's grandstanding crushed Ballard, and before long she was out of the group completely.

■ WESTLAWN CEMETERY

31472 Michigan Avenue, Wayne

Jackie Wilson, who collapsed onstage in 1975 and died in 1984, is buried in Westlawn Cemetery just outside Detroit. His pink mausoleum is inscribed "No More Lonely Teardrops."

The cemetery is open during daylight hours. Take Interstate 94 from the city toward the airport. Exit at Merriman Road and drive north to Michigan, then turn west. The phone number is 313-722-2530.

Flint

■ HOLIDAY INN

2207 West Bristol Road, Flint

Who drummer Keith Moon celebrated his twentieth birthday on August 23, 1967, but for drinking-age purposes, he decided to consider it his twenty-first birthday instead, and set about making the evening memorable. After the band's concert that night (they opened for Herman's Hermits at Atwood Stadium, a high school football field in Flint), everyone returned to the Holiday Inn and celebrated until midnight, when the motel manager came by and asked the boys to turn their record player down. A food fight ensued, and Moon emptied a fire extinguisher onto several cars in the parking lot, wrecked his room, jumped into the motel's empty swimming pool, tripped, stripped naked, fell, and broke two teeth. Then the police arrived. Moon's own account of this episode concludes with him driving a Lincoln Continental into the pool. This is the party that supposedly got the Who banned from the Holiday Inn chain for life.

The Holiday Inn is now a Days Inn. West Bristol intersects Interstate 75, the main highway from Detroit. The motel's phone number is 313-239-4686.

Kalamazoo

■ THE GIBSON GUITAR FACTORY

225 Parsons Street, Kalamazoo

Orville Gibson started his stringed-instrument business in Kalamazoo in the late nineteenth century. By early in the next century the company began to take off, and in 1917 Gibson moved to 225 Parsons Street. The factory stayed there until 1980, when it moved to Nashville.

Many fine acoustic guitars, mandolins, and banjos came out of this address over the years, but its greatest contribution to rock 'n' roll was the development and production of the Les Paul electric guitar, which was first introduced in 1952 and became the industry standard.

The building now holds a variety of commercial ventures, including Heritage Guitars.

Saginaw

■ NOT THE "96 TEARS" RECORDING SITE

1102 South Michigan Street, Saginaw

Evidence points to the old house at 1102 South Michigan as the recording location for "96 Tears." The garage-rock classic by ? and the Mysterians was supposedly recorded in March 1966 here, in the home (on the back porch, actually) of Lillie Gonzalez, the band's manager. The Mysterians were a hot local combo, popular among the Mexican-American population of the Flint-Saginaw-Bay City area. The song was released on the Pa-Go-Go label, shifted to Cameo, and became a number one hit.

Parts of this story are, alas, loco. Lillie Gonzalez claims that the band rehearsed and stayed at her house a lot, but she says the song was recorded in another now-forgotten house in Bay City.

Gonzalez's old house is now the office of Currie and Currie, a father-son law firm.

MINNESOTA

Chanhassen

■ PAISLEY PARK STUDIOS

7801 Audubon Road, Chanhassen

Prince invested wisely the millions that his movies and albums brought; he built Paisley Park, perhaps America's most photogenic recording facility. There are several gorgeous studio rooms here, a big soundstage for tour show rehearsals and video and movie production, and stacks of digitally perfect gear. The studio's discography is already significant. For example, Fine Young Cannibals' *The Raw and the Cooked* and R.E.M.'s *Out of Time* were recorded and mixed here. Of course, so was every recent song by Prince, who also shoots most of his videos on the lot.

Take Interstate 494 west from the Minneapolis Airport. In about fifteen minutes, exit onto Highway 5, which will take you toward Chanhassen. The studio, on Audubon Road, will come up on the south side of Highway 5. The area has many industrial-park style buildings; look for the one with little purple pyramids on the roof.

Hibbing

■ **BOB DYLAN'S BOYHOOD HOME**

2425 Seventh Avenue East, Hibbing

Dylan didn't become Dylan until after he left the old gray house in Hibbing, of course. Here he was Robert Zimmerman, a normal kid with an unremarkable life.

According to Chamber of Commerce officials, an intermittent trickle of tourists make their way to Hibbing, in search of Dylan's roots. When the Seventh Avenue property went up for sale a few years ago, it was even advertised in *Rolling Stone* magazine.

Minneapolis

■ **THE CC CLUB**

2600 Lyndale Avenue South, Minneapolis

The CC Club is a symbol of the rowdy Minneapolis rock 'n' roll sound of the Eighties, created by the likes of the Replacements and Hüsker Dü. For some reason, almost every rock magazine interview with Replacement leader

Paul Westerberg over a period of several years either was conducted here or mentioned the place.

Also worth mentioning is the Twin/Tone record company that's in the neighborhood. It started in Minneapolis in 1978 and was home base to the turn-that-noise-down! garage bands the Suburbs and Soul Asylum.

The CC Club isn't a music bar, per se, just a bar. The number is 612-874-7226.

■ CREATION AUDIO

2543 Nicollet Avenue South, Minneapolis

Founded in 1955 by recording pioneer Bruce Swedien (who's now one of Michael Jackson's closest studio collaborators), Creation Audio has produced many hits under several studio names. Polka music was the first major wave here. Then Bobby Vee came in to cut his hit, "Suzie Baby," and was followed by the Fendermen, whose "Mule Skinner Blues" loped into *Billboard*'s Top Ten. The studio reached its apogee in the mid-Sixties (the name was Kay Bank Studios then), when local phenomenon the Trashmen recorded the zany "Surfin' Bird." There have been many more significant songs made here, but none cooler. Well, maybe one: Dave Dudley's "Six Days on the Road," recorded here in 1963.

The studio still operates.

■ FIRST AVENUE/7TH STREET ENTRY

701 North First Avenue, Minneapolis

Prince was born and raised in Minneapolis, and the city is blanketed with Prince-related landmarks. The giant club on the corner of First and 7th was once called the Depot (the building was once a bus terminal), and its First Avenue side became famous as a principal setting in the 1984 movie *Purple Rain*. The place was a favorite spot of Prince's in the early Eighties. The smaller 7th Street Entry side is where local bands (and a few touring bands on the cusp) play.

Just about everywhere in Minneapolis, there are settings used in *Purple Rain* (over 10 million records sold, a soundtrack Oscar, and a half-million video cassettes). There's also the graffiti-covered overpass said to have inspired the *Graffiti Bridge* movie and soundtrack; and a host of private homes around the area in which Prince has lived, recorded, and thought sexy thoughts. One of Prince's post-success excesses open to the public is Glam Slam (110 North Fifth Street), a nightclub he built but apparently rarely visits.

Of course, Prince has spawned an entire school of Minneapolis funk peddlers. Jimmy Jam and Terry Lewis, architects of the Time sound as well as Janet Jackson's records, worked out of a studio at 4330 Nicollet, near downtown Minneapolis for a long time. They've since moved their top-secret Flyte Tyme operation elsewhere. Their old laboratory operates under new management and a new name, Entercor.

■ SOUND 80 STUDIOS

2709 East 25th Street, Minneapolis

Minneapolis' leading Seventies studio, Sound 80 saw the Doobie Brothers, Bob Dylan (he recut some *Blood on the Tracks* songs first laid down in New York), and Cat Stevens, among others. The studio had a nationwide reputation in those days for its technical prowess. One offshoot of that technomania was "Funkytown"—a 1980 hit for a group calling themselves Lipps, Inc.—which went to number one in forty countries and sold millions of copies.

Sound 80 still functions out of studios downtown, concentrating on commercial and broadcast-production work. The old 25th Street location closed in the mid-Eighties.

■ THE TEN O'CLOCK SCHOLAR

416 Fourteenth Avenue SE, Minneapolis

The Ten O'Clock Scholar, a campus haunt and folk club, was an important place for Bob Dylan during the few months he spent at the nearby University of Minnesota in 1959. Supposedly, the Scholar was the scene of two turning points in his life. First, he read *Bound for Glory*, the Woody Guthrie story, in one sitting at a table here. Second, on the night Bobby Zimmerman was about to perform for the first time at the Scholar and the manager asked him his name, the young singer blurted "Bob Dylan."

Since then, the Scholar's building has been razed and replaced by a Burger King.

Bobby Zimmerman's first official residence in Minneapolis was the Sigma Alpha Mu fraternity house, which has since been torn down and replaced by a new house at 925 University Avenue SE. It's painful to picture Bob Dylan as a fraternity man, but remember that he only stayed a few weeks.

Plymouth

■ K-TEL INTERNATIONAL

15535 Medina Road, Plymouth

Since the Sixties, K-Tel has specialized in packaging unlikely hit singles into even more unlikely hit albums, all marketed via off-hour television commercials. The company estimates sales of more than 100 million, which is impressive considering that most of those millions contained songs like "The Night Chicago Died," "Hocus Pocus," and "Love Grows (Where My Rosemary Goes)." Today, the company has branched into recording front-line artists and produces gospel and new age music.

MISSOURI

Kansas City

■ 12TH STREET AND VINE

12th and Vine Streets, Kansas City

Anybody who shows up at the corner of 12th Street and Vine hoping to find Wilbert Harrison's wine-and-women dreamland will be disappointed. It's not the same as it used to be, and had probably already started to fade when Harrison (in "Kansas City," a song credited to Jerry Leiber and Mike Stoller) made 12th and Vine into famous rock 'n' roll coordinates.

A trip here would not be wasted time, though. Kansas City is known to historians as a great jazz town, particularly during the wide-open days of the Twenties and Thirties. Count Basie (his jumping swing was a kindred spirit to rock 'n' roll) and bebop king Charlie Parker (who's buried in Lincoln Cemetery, on a hilltop about a half-hour east of town), just to name two, got their starts in Kansas City in those days, and their legacy is celebrated in a historic district at 18th and Vine. This neighborhood, now populated by public-housing projects, once boasted more than fifty nightclubs that remained open round the clock for two decades.

St. Louis

■ BERRY PARK

Buckner Road, Wentzville

Chuck Berry had grand plans to develop Berry Park, which opened in 1960 as a public swimming and fishing spot, into a full-fledged concert and recreation site. The park remains his home base, but he has yet to fulfill his vision. A few key scenes from *Hail, Hail Rock 'n' Roll,* the movie about Berry's life and work, were shot around the park, but the area is no longer open to the public.

Wentzville is a western exurb of St. Louis. To see the entrance to Berry's property, drive south from Interstate 70 on Highway Z (Church Street). As you pass Highway N, look for Buckner Road, then go west on Buckner.

■ BLUEBERRY HILL

6504 Delmar Boulevard, St. Louis

Blueberry Hill is a nightclub, a museum, a beer distributorship, a marketing enterprise, a restaurant, a local institution. Originally a little storefront joint in 1972, the Hill now occupies most of a city block. Co-owners Joe and Linda Edwards boast a personal collection of 30,000-plus singles, and Blueberry Hill's jukebox, a 2,000-title CD unit, regularly gets assigned the title "Best Jukebox in America" by one magazine or another. Joe Edwards also collects other things, including Fifties-through-Eighties effluvia, comic books, and neon signs.

Blueberry Hill sells tapes and CDs (Joe Edwards sponsors annual compilation discs by local talent), reference books (he's had to write a couple of them himself, just to keep track of his record collection), and beer (in 1981, Blueberry Hill started its own brand, Rock & Roll Beer, which is shipped to various parts of the country and overseas).

The club has an Elvis Presley exhibit and is also home to the original "Johnny B. Goode" guitar. Joe Edwards is a friend of Chuck Berry's, and the guitar on which the song was recorded, a gift from Berry, is on display.

Edwards launched the St. Louis Walk of Fame, and it's located just outside the club. It highlights favorite sons and daughters, including Josephine Baker, James "Cool Papa" Bell, Chuck Berry, William Burroughs, Miles Davis, Buddy Ebsen, T. S. Eliot, Betty Grable, Scott Joplin, Masters and Johnson, Stan Musial, Marlon Perkins, Vincent Price, Tina Turner, and Tennessee Williams.

Blueberry Hill, which opens at 11 A.M. every day, is in the section of town known as University City. The phone number is 314-727-0880.

■ RIVERPORT AMPHITHEATER

Interstate 70, outside St. Louis

Guns 'n' Roses christened the outdoor Riverport in the band's own special way on July 2, 1991: during the concert, lead singer Axl Rose spotted an audience member with a camera and leaped into the crowd. The subsequent riot resulted in some sixty injuries, sixteen arrests, and roughly $200,000 in damages to the amphitheater. Rose lost a contact lens.

The Riverport is in Maryland Heights, about 25 minutes from St. Louis on Interstate 70. Call 314-298-9944 for ticket information.

Springfield

■ THE FEDERAL MEDICAL CENTER

1900 West Sunshine Street, Springfield

Chuck Berry was incarcerated in the Federal Medical Center in the early Sixties, after his Mann Act conviction. Berry didn't just waste time doing time, but took classes to finish his high school degree and learned to type—and began work on his notorious autobiography, which he worked on over the next twenty years. He also wrote "No Particular Place to Go," "The Promised Land," and several other ironic songs. Berry claims in his autobiography that he had a brief encounter with the Birdman of Alcatraz, Richard Stroud, during his stay here. Berry was released in October 1963, after serving about two years of his three-year sentence.

The Medical Center houses sick federal prisoners and is located on the southwest side of Springfield, near the intersection of Springfield Avenue and the Kansas Expressway.

NEBRASKA

Omaha

■ THE OMAHA HILTON

1616 Dodge Street, Omaha

Grand Funk, touring America in February 1973, stayed at the Omaha Hilton, and supposedly it was an incident at the hotel that inspired the verse from the immortal single, "We're An American Band":

> Four young chiquitas in Omaha
> Waiting for the band to return from the show,
> Feeling good, feeling right, it's Saturday night,
> The hotel detective, he was out of sight,

These fine ladies, they had a plan,
They was out to meet the boys in the band,
They said, "Come on, dudes, let's get it on,"
And we proceeded to tear that hotel down.

When the song became a hit, Omaha newspaper columnist Peter Citron checked with hotel management and was told that nothing unusual happened during Grand Funk's stay, and that, in fact, a much greater ruckus was caused when the Osmond Brothers booked some rooms here. Citron also discovered that the concert was on a Sunday, not a Saturday.

Grand Funk drummer Don Brewer, who wrote the tune, confirms the suspicion that "American Band" was penned solely to capture the spirit of life on the road for a rock band, and that it was never meant to be perceived literally.

By the way, some commentators have credited "We're an American Band" with introducing the phrase "party down" ("We'll come into your town/We'll help you party down") into the popular lexicon.

The Hilton is now called the Red Lion Hotel, and rates range from $69 to $112. The phone number is 402-346-7600.

OHIO

Cincinnati

■ RIVERFRONT COLISEUM

100 Broadway, Cincinnati

Eleven fans of the Who died at the Riverfront Coliseum in a preconcert stampede on December 3, 1979.

The Coliseum books family shows, sports, and a few concerts. There is no monument or plaque commemorating the Who dead. The phone number for ticket information is 513-241-1818.

*After the tragic stampede at a Who concert, where eleven people died
(Riverfront Coliseum, Cincinnati, Ohio)*

Cleveland

■ THE CLEVELAND ARENA

3717 Euclid Avenue, Cleveland

Even disc jockey/promoter Alan Freed was amazed by the response to his first Moondog Balls—live shows featuring the independent-label performers whose music he played on WJW—many of which were held at the Cleveland Arena in the early Fifties. One such event drew 25,000, although the Arena's capacity was half that. Freed would continue the Moondog Ball tradition when he moved to New York in 1954.

The arena has been demolished, and the lot now holds the Cleveland Red Cross headquarters.

■ RECORD RENDEZVOUS

---

300 Prospect SE, Cleveland

In 1951, Record Rendezvous owner Leo Mintz noticed local teens buying "race" records—rhythm and blues songs by black artists—at his store. After Mintz demonstrated the phenomenon to Alan Freed, who was hosting a beautiful-music radio program on Cleveland's WJW, Freed convinced station management to let him play the records on the air. Freed's "Moondog Rock 'n' Roll Party" started in June 1951.

The Rendezvous stayed in business until the mid-Eighties, when it became a furniture store.

■ THE ROCK 'N' ROLL HALL OF FAME

North Coast Harbor and East 9th Street, Cleveland

Cleveland, whose only true claim to rock 'n' roll prominence (Alan Freed) left for New York in the mid-Fifties, was picked as home to the Hall of Fame in the mid-Eighties, after the city mounted a massive petition drive and made promises of local funding. The hall's New York-based governing board has been inducting members since 1986, although the hall does not yet exist as a physical structure. Architect I. M. Pei has submitted a design, and completion is expected in the late Nineties.

■ WJW

One Playhouse Square Building, 1375 Euclid Avenue, Cleveland

Alan Freed began broadcasting "The Moondog Rock 'n' Roll Party" over WJW radio in June 1951. Credited with popularizing the term "rock 'n' roll," Freed had a mixed audience from the beginning: teens, both black and white, loved the music. Freed's riotous shtick included slapping a telephone book in rhythm with the records he played and occasionally guzzling Scotch during shows. WJW had a clear 50,000-watt signal in those days, so the show's influence around the Midwest was enormous. Freed, whose career would be ruined by the payola scandals later in the decade, left Cleveland for the big time (New York's WINS) in 1954.

WJW radio is vapor (the call letters live on in one of Cleveland's TV outlets, which broadcasts from elsewhere), but a small plaque near the building's entrance commemorates its place in rock 'n' roll history.

Columbus

■ HOLIDAY INN

---

175 East Town Street, Columbus

On March 16, 1979, Elvis Costello and his band were drinking in the Columbus Holiday Inn's bar with Bonnie Bramlett and the Stephen Stills Band. Costello, intoxicated (as were most of the participants) and reportedly provoked by some Brit-bashing on the part of the Americans present, made belligerent, racial slurs about Ray Charles and James Brown. Bonnie decked him. Costello is among the more brilliant performers and songwriters of his time, but he spent most of the Eighties trying to explain that evening to interviewers.

The place is now the Quality Hotel/City Center. The phone number is 614-861-3281 and rooms go for about $60.

Kent

■ **KENT STATE UNIVERSITY**

Highway 59, East of Akron

On May 4, 1970, Ohio National Guardsmen fired into a crowd of Kent State students who were protesting the Vietnam war; four were killed. America's musicians mobilized: Neil Young wrote, recorded, and released "Ohio" within the next few weeks and Marvin Gaye produced "What's Going On" the following year. Joe Walsh was an English major at the university at the time and witnessed the shootings. Later, he campaigned to have an on-campus memorial erected to the slain and wounded.

WISCONSIN

East Troy

■ **ALPINE VALLEY MUSIC THEATER**

State Highway D, outside East Troy

Blues guitarist Stevie Ray Vaughan played his last concert at Alpine Valley, on August 26, 1990. Eric Clapton, Buddy Guy, Robert Cray, and Vaughan's brother, Jimmie, also performed that evening. Minutes after the concert ended, Vaughan, a pilot, and three members of Clapton's entourage died in a helicopter crash.

Vaughan took the final seat in the five-seat helicopter shortly after midnight. Flying in heavy fog, the aircraft hit a 1,000-foot ski hill about three-quarters of a mile southeast of the theater.

Alpine Valley, which schedules concerts all summer, is on State Highway

Kent State massacre—May 4, 1970 (Kent, Ohio)

D, five miles outside East Troy, which is about an hour's drive southwest of Milwaukee. There is no access to the crash site. The management of the Alpine Valley ski resort, which is not affiliated with the concert hall, has yet to erect any kind of marker or monument where the chopper went down—primarily because the crash site is on a ski run. And, of course, the ski resort is private property, which means you have to stay off in summer. But winter is a different story. Buy a lift ticket and ride the chair lift to the top of the Mohawk run. As you near the top, look down and to your left. There it was.

Madison

■ OTIS REDDING CRASH SITE

Lake Monona, Madison

A plane carrying Otis Redding crashed into Lake Monona on the afternoon of December 10, 1967. Redding and the Bar Kays (his backup band and Stax label mates) were traveling from a performance in Cleveland to do two shows that night in Madison. Weather conditions were poor—there was a light drizzle falling through heavy fog—and the plane was on landing approach to the Madison airport when it went down. The exact cause of the accident was never determined. Witnesses at the scene said they could hear the plane's engine sputtering, although no distress call was made to the Madison tower. One Bar Kay, Ben Cauley, survived the wreck.

All of the bodies were eventually recovered. (It's a dearly held legend around Madison that the bodies were never brought to the surface; area boaters sometimes blame motor malfunctions on "Otis.") Redding is buried near Macon, Georgia.

A sweet little Otis Redding memorial was erected on the western shore of Lake Monona in the late Eighties: three benches and a plaque in lakefront Law Park (on John Nolan Drive), which is not far from the Wisconsin State Capitol building. If you sit on the middle bench and face approximately to the east overlooking the lake, you're pointed in the general direction of the crash.

Milwaukee

■ ORIENTAL DRUGS

2238 North Farwell Street, Milwaukee

The Pretenders were booked to perform at Milwaukee's Oriental Theater in the summer of 1981. On the afternoon before the show, one of the band members noticed the Violent Femmes (local purveyors of acoustic new wave) playing for spare change on the sidewalk between the theater and

Violent Femmes, in front of the Downer Theater (Milwaukee, Wisconsin)

© Mary C. Jones

Oriental Drugs. Soon, Chrissie Hynde, the Pretenders' leader, was listening, too. When the Femmes' set concluded, Hynde asked if they wanted to open that night's concert. They did, and have since gone on to considerable underground success around the world. Modern Milwaukee residents consider the band their greatest musical export. (The Pretenders are still popular, too.)

Though the Oriental Theater has been cut up into several smaller movie houses, Oriental Drugs remains as it was on the Femmes' big day. And buskers still play for change in front of the place.

THE SOUTHWEST

ARIZONA

Kingman

■ **OLD ROUTE 66**

Topock through Oatman to Kingman, Peach Springs, and Seligman

Once the main road west, Route 66 was killed off by jet planes and the interstates. A vintage 160-mile section of "The Main Street of America" centers on Kingman and is maintained by the state of Arizona as an historic road. Believe it or not, this stretch of asphalt is becoming a major international tourist attraction. A celebration (with classic car rally) is held every April.

Call 602-753-5001 (the number of the Kingman-based Historic Route 66 Association of Arizona) for a complete rundown.

Phoenix

■ **AUDIO RECORDERS**

3703 North 7th Street, Phoenix

Duane Eddy recorded his biggest hits, including "Moving 'n' Grooving," "Ramrod," and "Rebel Rouser" at Audio Recorders—where an old water tank supplied an awesome echo effect. In 1964 the studio moved to 3830 North 7th Street, and there Dyke and the Blazers cut the original version of "Funky Broadway."

The old building at 3703 was torn down and has been replaced by offices. But the studio (now called Audio Video Recorders) remains busy.

■ BROADWAY ROAD

Off Central Avenue, Phoenix

Dyke and the Blazers were habitues of the rough bars and after-hours clubs along Broadway Road at the time they cut the original "Funky Broadway" in the mid-Sixties. (Later, Wilson Pickett scored a hit with a cover version that put a finger-popping spin on the gritty, menacing original.) Some rock 'n' roll historians claim "Funky Broadway" introduced "funky" to the popular vocabulary.

Broadway is a major east-west thoroughfare through the south side of town and crosses Central Avenue.

■ THE VIP CLUB

4133 North 7th Street, Phoenix

The VIP Club was actually a rented Jaycees hall. In the mid-Sixties its house band, the Spiders (their specialty was covering Rolling Stones tunes), were already developing a theatrical act: the band would dress in black and play behind a "web" made of clothesline. The lead singer was young Vincent Furnier—who later went on to stardom with a name conjured up one night on a Ouija board: Alice Cooper.

In later years the Red, White, and Blues Band, an early version of the Tubes, played the room.

Tempe

■ SUN DEVIL STADIUM

Arizona State University, Tempe

A typical college-football stadium, Sun Devil has also been the site of several concerts which were filmed for posterity. In December 1981, the Rolling Stones used the stadium to film segments of their movie *Let's Spend the Night Together*, and the outdoor performance scenes in Barbra Streisand's version of *A Star Is Born* were shot here in March 1976. U2 played at Sun Devil in 1987, and the lonely-cowboy atmosphere of Tempe's damp nights was captured in *Rattle and Hum*.

The stadium is located north of campus on the south bank of the dry Salt River.

COLORADO

Aspen

■ THE HARD ROCK CAFE

210 South Galena Street, Aspen

S ki slopes are visible from the front door of the Aspen Hard Rock Cafe, so it's not surprising that the memorabilia collection leans toward the downhill. In addition to the skis, boots, and poles of the famous on display, the restaurant also has guitars used by John Denver, k. d. lang, and the Nitty Gritty Dirt Band, and features many Buddy Holly items.

The phone number is 303-920-1666.

Denver

■ MILE HIGH STADIUM

2755 West Seventeenth Avenue, Denver

M ile High Stadium was the scene of the three-day Denver Pop Festival in June 1969. Joe Cocker, Creedence Clearwater Revival, Jimi Hendrix, Iron Butterfly, and Frank Zappa and the Mothers were among the headliners. The last two nights of the festival concluded with the crowd awash in tear gas, and the closing concert would be the last public performance of the Jimi Hendrix Experience.

Mile High specializes in sporting events, especially Denver Broncos games. The number is 303-458-4848.

Red Rocks Park, outside Denver

An outdoor amphitheater set in stunning natural stone formations, Red Rocks is probably one of most aesthetic concert spots on the continent. It officially opened in 1941, but the site had been used as a natural amphitheater for many years before that. The Beatles played here in August 1964; songs from a rainy U2 concert, in June 1983, were captured on video and released as *Under a Blood Red Sky*. The dramatic footage got heavy play on MTV; this is considered one of the band's big breaks.

Red Rocks offers concerts all summer, but it's worth seeing just for itself. Call 303-572-4700 for more information.

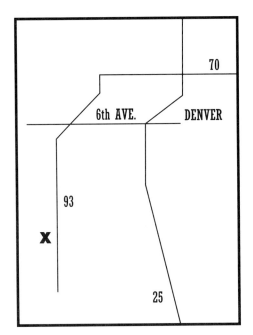

Red Rocks

NEVADA

Las Vegas

■ THE ALADDIN HOTEL

3667 Las Vegas Boulevard South, Las Vegas

Elvis Presley's omnipresent manager, Colonel Parker, was a friend of Aladdin Hotel owner Milton Prell, so it was here that Elvis married Priscilla Beaulieu on May 1, 1967. The wedding entourage flew in from Palm Springs on a Lear jet a few hours before the ceremony, and Elvis and his bride-to-be got their marriage license from the Clark County Clerk's office at about 3:30 A.M. The eight-minute ceremony took place in Prell's personal suite at 9:41 A.M. After a brief reception and press conference, the wedding party returned to Palm Springs.

You can sleep in the room where Elvis got married. It's now known as the Executive Suite, and depending on the season and economic conditions, the two modest rooms rent for anywhere from $95 a night. The room's number is 363. Call 702-736-0111 for reservations.

■ THE FLAMINGO

3555 Las Vegas Boulevard South, Las Vegas

During a summer 1967 Supremes engagement at the Flamingo, Motown boss Berry Gordy shuffled Cindy Birdsong into—and Florence Ballard out of—the group's lineup.

The Flamingo is now known as the Flamingo Hilton, where the phone number is 702-733-3111.

Elvis ties the knot, 1967 (Las Vegas)

▪ THE FRONTIER HOTEL

3120 Las Vegas Boulevard South, Las Vegas

In 1956 the Strip was not ready for the Pelvis, and Elvis Presley's engagement in the Frontier Hotel's Venus Room was a disaster. After a few performances, comedian Shecky Greene was bumped ahead of Presley on the bill.

Also, during a stand at the Frontier in January 1970, Diana Ross officially left the Supremes.

The Venus Room is now a restaurant. The hotel's reservations number is 702-794-8200.

▪ GRACELAND WEDDING CHAPEL

619 Las Vegas Boulevard South, Las Vegas

Jon Bon Jovi got married at the Graceland Wedding Chapel. The top-of-the-line package costs $150. Call 702-382-0091.

▪ THE HARD ROCK CAFE

4475 Paradise Road, Las Vegas

The sign in front of the Vegas Hard Rock Cafe—a huge Les Paul guitar—is a preview of things to come, for here is where the Hard Rock people are building a hotel and casino.

Highlights from the restaurant's collection include guitars from Elvis Presley, Johnny Cash, James Burton, Stevie Ray Vaughan, Eric Clapton, and Billy Zoom. Also featured are platform boots worn by Rufus Thomas in his Funky Chicken phase, a microphone from the Star Club in Hamburg, Germany, a superb Roy Orbison collection, and a display case containing eyeglasses once worn by Buddy Holly, Roy Orbison, and Elvis Presley.

Call 702-733-8400 for details.

■ THE LAS VEGAS HILTON

3000 Paradise Road, Las Vegas

Elvis Presley staged his live comeback at the International Hotel (since renamed the Las Vegas Hilton) in 1969, and the hotel became Presley's home base in Vegas for the rest of his life. The thirtieth-floor room he stayed in, once known as the Imperial Suite, is now called the Elvis Presley Suite. Colonel Parker kept a room elsewhere in the hotel.

The suite is usually reserved for the Hilton's showroom headliner, but it couldn't hurt to ask. Call 702-732-5111.

■ THE SAHARA HOTEL

2535 Las Vegas Boulevard South, Las Vegas

The Beatles came to town for a blistering day and night in August 1964. They played two shows in the Rotunda of the Las Vegas Convention Center (the saucer-shaped building has since been torn down) and stayed in suites on the eighteenth floor of the Sahara Hotel. For kicks, they had hotel management bring slot machines up to their rooms. They also met with Liberace and Pat Boone.

NEW MEXICO

Clovis

■ NORMAN PETTY STUDIOS

1313 West 7th Street, 206 Main Street, Clovis

Norman Petty, a Clovis native, started out as a keyboardist and bandleader and eventually moved into the recording business. His little studio on 7th Street is famous for its recordings of Buddy Holly, who came to Clovis after a failed attempt to make country records in Nashville. Most of the songs for which Holly is remembered—including "That'll Be the Day" and "Peggy

Sue"—were cut here. A not-quite-true legend has it that Holly and his young band were working at Petty's when the sound of a chirping cricket interrupted the session, thus inspiring the combo's name. The site also produced the top song of 1963, Jerry Gilmer and the Fireballs' "Sugar Shack."

In 1968, Petty bought an old movie house on Main Street closer to downtown Clovis and moved his setup there. Today, it remains a functioning studio, mostly booking dates for radio ads.

The original Petty studio on West 7th Street has been partially restored and is opened for tours on special occasions, such as Clovis' annual music festival. Call the Main Street studio for information, at 505-763-7565.

Taos

■ **THE *EASY RIDER* JAIL CELL**

Michael McCormick Gallery, 121-B North Plaza

The jail scenes in *Easy Rider* (the ones where Peter Fonda and Dennis Hopper meet Jack Nicholson) were shot in the old courthouse in Taos. Now it's an art gallery. A small plaque and a few movie stills attest to the room's role in cinematic history.

OKLAHOMA

Tulsa

■ CAIN'S BALLROOM

423 North Main Street, Tulsa

Built in 1924 for ballroom dancing, Cain's later became a concert hall and was one of the stops on the Sex Pistols' tour of America in 1978. But even more importantly, Cain's was home to the Bob Wills and the Texas Playboys radio show, which was broadcast from the Thirties through the Fifties. Wills, who did a live show every day (plus Thursday and Saturday nights) for many years, was a pioneering bandleader whose western swing—heavy with jazz and blues influences—reached the *world* via Tulsa's mighty KVOO.

Cain's is still a concert hall, and retains much of its Thirties charm. Call 918-584-2309.

TEXAS

Amarillo

■ THE CADILLAC RANCH

Interstate 40, west of Amarillo

The ranch is a powerful art statement: ten Cadillacs buried tailfin-up in a farm field. The cars were planted in June 1974 by Doug Michels, Hudson Marquez, and Chip Lord (with funding from eccentric Texan Stanley March III), and are arranged chronologically from 1948 to 1963. View it all from the interstate (formerly the path of the fabled Route 66), or stop and take a closer look. Thousands of visitors have carved their names into the cars' metal hides, and Bruce Springsteen carved the ranch into pop-music history by featuring a song about it on his album *The River.*

Austin

■ ANTONE'S

2915 Guadalupe Street, Austin

Antone's is one of those world-famous nightclubs. Its big breakout came in the late Seventies, when the Fabulous Thunderbirds were the house band. Stevie Ray Vaughan played here a lot, too.

Call 512-474-5314 for show information.

■ ARMADILLO WORLD HEADQUARTERS (ARMADILLO WHQ)

503½ Barton Springs Road, Austin

Armadillo was an old Texas State Guard Armory and an important site in the development of the outlaw country-rocker school of music. Here, in the early Seventies, Willie Nelson became a crossover phenomenon attracting both hippies and rednecks to the same venue. Willie's first Fourth of July picnic/concert/party in 1972 was his way of bringing everyone together.

The place was torn down in the early Eighties and replaced by a thirteen-story office building called One Texas Center.

■ THREADGILL'S

6416 North Lamar Boulevard, Austin

Janis Joplin performed at Threadgill's as a University of Texas student in the early Sixties; today, the club displays some of her gold records and many photos. Run by Eddie Wilson, once the owner of Armadillo WHQ, Threadgill's is still a popular setting for music. The number is 512-451-5440.

■ WALK OF STARS

6th and Brazos Streets, Austin

Set at the foot of the Driskill Hotel, the Walk of Stars honors some of the state's talent, including Willie Nelson and Janis Joplin. The walk isn't limited to musicians, though—football coaches and astronauts also have stars.

The walk will eventually head up Trinity to 6th and then run along 6th (which has many music clubs) between Congress Street and Interstate 35.

Beaumont

■ THE BIG BOPPER'S GRAVE

Forest Lawn Memorial Park, 4955 Pine Street, Beaumont

J. P. Richardson, better known as "the Big Bopper," rests under a bronze marker near the funeral home in Forest Lawn Memorial Park.

The cemetery is at the north end of town. Call 409-892-5912 for hours and information.

Dallas / Fort Worth

■ CARDI'S

Medallion Plaza, 6400 East Northwest Highway, Dallas

Around midnight on April 12, 1982, David Crosby was caught free-basing in the backstage dressing room of Cardi's, a Dallas nightclub. The arresting officer also found a loaded .45-caliber pistol in Crosby's possession.

In lieu of prison, a judge sent Crosby to a drug rehabilitation facility in Summit, New Jersey. He soon skipped out of Fair Oaks, had other run-ins with the law, and ultimately served time in the Texas State Penitentiary.

■ THE HARD ROCK CAFE

2601 McKinney Avenue, Dallas

Jimi Hendrix and ZZ Top dominate the memorabilia in the Dallas Hard Rock. A Hendrix-owned Gibson Flying V hangs on one wall; the original fuzzy guitars used by ZZ Top in their video for "Legs" hang on another. Call 214-855-0007.

■ ST. MARK'S SCHOOL OF TEXAS

10600 Preston Road, Dallas

Boz Scaggs and Steve Miller met as preppies at tradition-rich St. Mark's in the late Fifties. They both left before graduating, but later teamed up again at the University of Wisconsin in Madison and formed the Steve Miller Blues Band.

DeKalb

■ RICK NELSON DEATH SITE

Near FM Road 990, outside DeKalb

Rick Nelson—Fifties' child star and country-rock pioneer—and his band were flying to a New Year's Eve job in Dallas on December 31, 1985, when an onboard fire forced the plane to crash-land in a field outside DeKalb. The pilot and copilot survived, but Nelson, his fiance, and five others were killed when the DC3 exploded on the ground.

Take Highway 82 east out of town. Cross the railroad tracks to FM Road 1840. FM road 990 comes up in about a half-mile; turn right onto it. The crash site is 300 to 400 yards west of 990, about a half-mile from the intersection of 1840 and 990.

Del Rio

■ ROSWELL HOTEL

137 West Garfield Street, Del Rio

Wolfman Jack (real name: Bob Smith) kept a room at the Roswell Hotel during his tenure as operator and star of XERF, one of the fabled border-radio giants. Broadcasting just over the Mexican border across from Del Rio—and therefore outside the jurisdiction of American communications authorities—XERF had a more powerful transmitter than American stations were allowed, and its signal could be picked up all over the continent. (The Wolfman got personal-appearance requests all the way from Kansas.) Russia tuned in, too, and once tried to block XERF's signal after the Wolfman criticized Khrushchev.

The station's broadcast day included religious programming, endless advertisements for such items as diet pills, rhythm and blues records, and cases of live baby chicks (100 for $3.95), and, around midnight every night, the outrageous Wolfman. His shows introduced thousands of American teenagers to the forbidden thrills of early R & B and rock. When ZZ Top sings about hearing it on the "X," they're talking about the wild sounds lobbed across the border by the Mexican radio pirates.

There's a story about the Roswell Hotel. Sometime in the mid- to late Fifties, it goes, the Wolfman was in the middle of an intimate encounter with the Wolfwoman in his suite (and conscientiously monitoring the station at the same time). Suddenly, angry Spanish words and sounds of violence came over the radio: outlaws were taking over the station. The Wolfman interrupted his lovemaking, rounded up a posse of local mercenaries, and forcibly reclaimed the studio and transmitter tower.

Later in his career, after he had moved his act to XERB near Tijuana, the Wolfman was heard by the teen cruisers in tiny Modesto, California. One of them was young George Lucas, who went on to craft *American Graffiti*—which is in large part a tribute to the magic of the Wolfman's border-radio music.

The Roswell Hotel still stands, looking just as it did in the Wolfman days, although the building has been turned into apartments. Six stories tall and vintage 1928, the hotel has hosted several characters, including (according to a staff member there) Elvis Presley and John Wayne. The phone number is 512-774-4029.

Houston

■ CITY AUDITORIUM

615 Louisiana Street, Houston

Johnny Ace killed himself backstage at the City Auditorium on Christmas Eve, 1954, playing Russian roulette—according to the official story. The unofficial story hints at foul play. Ace, who was only in his mid-twenties at the time, had already built a considerable career working with B. B. King's Beale Streeters combo and likely was headed to stardom as an R & B singer.

The 3,000-seat auditorium, which has been renovated and renamed the Jones Hall for the Performing Arts, is home to the Houston Symphony. The phone number is 713-853-8000.

■ GOLD STAR STUDIOS

5626 Brock Street, Houston

Gold Star Studios was home base for producer Huey "Crazy Cajun" Meaux, creator of much funky Texas R & B, blues, and rock 'n' roll music. Meaux, who first launched his recording business out of his barber shop in Winnie, Texas, produced R & B hits by Jivin' Gene, Joe Barry, and Barbara Lynn, and many more releases on the Duke-Peacock independent label. Later, he attempted to cash in on the British Invasion by building a band around San Antonio's Doug Sahm. He called the group the Sir Douglas Quintet, and "She's About a Mover," recorded here on Brock Street in 1965, was a blast of Tex-Mex honk. Meaux also recorded some of B. J. Thomas' first songs, the Big Bopper's "Chantilly Lace," and all of Freddie Fender's hits—including "Wasted Days and Wasted Nights."

The studio is now called Sugar Hill, but Huey Meaux is still on the job.

■ THE HARD ROCK CAFE

2801 Kirby Drive, Houston

ach Hard Rock takes pains to honor local heroes, and Houston's does not disappoint. In the lobby is a beautiful ZZ Top display, with guitars from Dusty Hill and Billy Gibbons and a snare from Frank Beard, and a "God Bless Roy Orbison" tribute. The Texas Wall features items from Jimmy Vaughan, Joe Ely, Charlie Sexton, and Willie Nelson. (They've also got one of Alan Shepard's golf clubs here. Get it?)

Call 713-520-1134 for hours and information.

Huntsville

■ TEXAS DEPARTMENT OF CRIMINAL JUSTICE FACILITY

FM Road 2821, Huntsville

avid Crosby served most of his mid-Eighties jail sentence for gun and drug possession in the Criminal Justice Facility at Huntsville, where he worked in the prison's mattress factory.

Crosby was kept in what is known as the Wynne unit, which had a reputation for having the best inmate rock band. He claims prison wasn't so bad.

La Grange

■ THE CHICKEN RANCH

Off Highway 71, La Grange

n operation since the early part of the century, the Chicken Ranch brothel was famous long before ZZ Top's commemoration of it in their 1973 song "La Grange." The ranch closed in the Seventies, but its buildings were preserved and relocated to Dallas where they became a disco.

Highway 71 is known as the Texas Independence Trail. The ranch was on a gravel road about a quarter-mile off 71, two miles east of La Grange.

Lubbock

■ THE COTTON CLUB

Slaton Highway, outside Lubbock

Elvis Presley was a regular attraction at the Cotton Club roadhouse/dance hall in 1955. Buddy Holly saw Presley's first show there and was the opening act for his next appearance. In fact, on that second trip, Buddy and his "Western and Bop" partner Bob Montgomery met Presley's bus at the edge of town and gave Elvis a personal tour of Lubbock. The Cotton Club also was supposedly the site of Holly's discovery by a Nashville talent scout.

The club is located on Highway 84, two and a half miles west of Lubbock's city limits. The owners still book country acts most weekends. Call 806-745-4277.

■ BUDDY HOLLY'S GRAVE

Lubbock Cemetery, Quirt and 31st Streets, Lubbock

Buddy Holly's parents brought him home to Lubbock after the plane crash in Clear Lake, Iowa. His grave marker is flat and inscribed with a relief of his Fender guitar. (His name is "Holley" on the stone, which is the correct spelling. Someone mistakenly dropped the "e" when drawing up Buddy's first record contract, and he stuck with that version for the rest of his life.) The marker is the second one on the site; the original was stolen. Visitors often leave guitar picks at the grave.

The cemetery is on the edge of town, near the intersection of Quirt and 31st. Once inside, stay to the right on the cemetery road marked Azalea. The grave is on your left, about 100 feet from where the road forks. An evergreen tree stands about thirty feet away.

ABOVE: Buddy Holly gravesite (Lubbock, Texas)

RIGHT: Buddy Holly statue (Lubbock)

Buddy Holly sites around Lubbock:
1) The statue
2) The grave
3) The Cotton Club

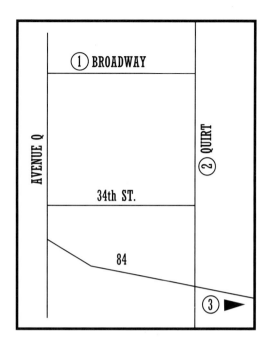

Favorite Son

Lubbock was Buddy Holly's home virtually all his life, and the town is committed to honoring his memory. As you view the modern civic center, keep in mind that the city mothers and fathers did not erect a statue of a prominent oil man, cotton farmer, state legislator, or Old West pioneer (they already had a statue of Old West pioneers) there. No, they picked a guitar-playing rock 'n' roller who sang with the hiccups.

The local Buddy Holly Memorial Society helps organize an annual birthday celebration during the first week of September. The telephone number is 806-799-4299. In addition, Lubbock's Chamber of Commerce (806-763-4666) answers questions and offers a free brochure of every site in town relevant to Buddy's life.

■ **THE BUDDY HOLLY STATUE**
8th Street and Avenue Q

The Buddy Holly Statue is among the best-known rock 'n' roll landmarks anywhere. The 2,500-pound bronze, created by sculptor Grant Speed, was unveiled (to coincide with the local premiere of *The Buddy Holly Story*) in May 1979. The bronze Buddy hunches over his guitar at the center of a round concrete podium. and plaques honoring other West Texas musicians (including Joe Ely, Roy Orbison, Bob Wills, Tanya Tucker, a few of the Crickets, and the Gatlin Brothers) are displayed around the perimeter of the base. Lubbock calls this its Walk of Fame.

The statue is nestled in a small canyon between a La Quinta Inn and a Holiday Inn. Parking is available at the nearby motels and civic-center buildings.

■ BUDDY'S FIRST HOME
1911 6th Street

Buddy's first house, once located at this address, was saved from demolition by a local fan who bought the place and moved it to the edge of town. Its new location is kept secret.

■ BUDDY'S SCHOOLS

Buddy attended J. T. Hutchinson Junior High (3102 Canton Street) and Lubbock High (2004 19th Street). Both are still around.

■ KDAV STUDIO
6602 Quirt Street

In 1953, Holly and his friend Bob Montgomery broadcast a weekly radio show from the KDAV studio, which now houses KRLB. The boys named their combo Buddy and Bob, and called their music show "Western and Bop."

■ TABERNACLE BAPTIST CHURCH
1911 34th Street

Buddy was baptized at the Tabernacle Baptist Church. It's still around, too.

■ ROADHOUSE TRANSPORTATION

1725 North Nashville Street

Roadhouse is one of the leading suppliers of road-ready touring buses for rock, pop, and country acts. ZZ Top, Madonna, Billy Idol, Janet Jackson, and Frank Sinatra have all been customers.

Port Arthur

■ MUSEUM OF THE GULF COAST

Gates Memorial Library, Lamar University, 317 Stilwell Boulevard, Port Arthur

The Museum of the Gulf Coast is a little out of the way, but it has a fine American Pop Culture Exhibit that pays special attention to Texans who've made it big in show business. And it's an especially good place to get an overview of the local country, jazz, blues, and rock 'n' roll talent—Janis Joplin, J. P. Richardson (the Big Bopper), Johnny and Edgar Winter, Ivory Joe Hunter, Harry James, Tex Ritter, George Jones, and many more.

Joplin grew up in Port Arthur, but little remains from her life here. Her childhood home was torn down years ago, so the best bet for making any Joplin/Port Arthur linkage is to stop at the museum.

The museum is in the process of moving to a new site at 700 Proctor Street. Call 409-983-4921 for more information.

Rusk

■ TEXAS STATE HOSPITAL

Highway 69, Rusk

Roky Erickson, psychedelic tyro and leader of the 13th Floor Elevators, spent three years in the late Sixties at the Texas State Hospital after pleading insanity to marijuana-possession charges.

Still a state psychiatric hospital, the place holds about 450 patients. Rusk is about 120 miles from Dallas on Highway 69. The buildings are visible from the highway.

San Antonio

■ BLUE BONNET HOTEL

St. Mary's and Pecan Streets, San Antonio

It's probable that blues great Robert Johnson cut most of his famous recordings in a makeshift studio erected in the Blue Bonnet Hotel, back in 1936. Those recordings made history; Eric Clapton, especially, was moved by Johnson's eerie guitar playing. As mentioned earlier, the compact-disc reissue of the songs in the early Nineties made the pop charts and went gold.

The Blue Bonnet bit the dust in 1988, but Robert Johnson lives on.

South Padre Island

■ BILL HALEY'S FINAL RESTING PLACE

The Gulf of Mexico, near South Padre Island

In his last years, Bill Haley was tormented by delusions and paranoia. After he died (in Harlingen, Texas, on February 9, 1981), his body was cremated in nearby Brownsville, and his ashes were later scattered from an airplane flying above the Gulf.

Waxahachie

■ SOUTHWESTERN BIBLE INSTITUTE

1200 Sycamore Street, Waxahachie

In the early Fifties, Jerry Lee Lewis was expelled from the Southwestern Bible Institute after just three months as a divinity student. Seems he was asked to play a hymn one night during chapel services, and responded by pumping out a Killer version.

During his numbered days here, Lewis spent most of his leisure time sneaking away to the many joints in nearby Dallas.

The institution is now called Southwestern Assemblies of God College. Call 214-937-4010.

Wink

■ ROY ORBISON MUSEUM

---

205 East Hendricks Boulevard, Wink

Roy Orbison spent his youth in Wink, and the town is making some moves to commemorate that fact. So far, the museum—a storefront on Wink's main street—is mostly a gift shop, but there are plans to expand it into a display of Orbison artifacts. The town also plans to erect a monument to Orbison, for which a fund-raising drive is now underway.

Call Wink's city hall at 915-527-3441 to check on the museum's progress. Also ask for details on the town's annual Orbison festival, held the first weekend in June.

THE WEST

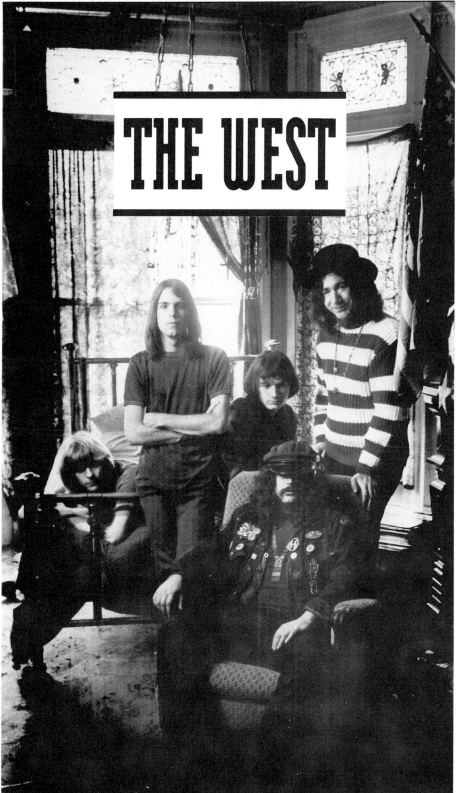

SOUTHERN CALIFORNIA

Burbank

■ NBC STUDIOS

3000 West Alameda Avenue, Burbank

When Elvis Presley filmed his Singer Christmas TV special at the NBC studios in the summer of 1968, the event was not without hitches. Colonel Parker, Presley's Svengali, had wanted the show to be a cornball salute to the holiday, but producer Steve Binder put the star in black leather and made him sing rockabilly again. The Colonel, meanwhile, was sent out to distribute tickets to the tapings, which for some reason he neglected to do. At the last minute Binder had to run to a nearby Bob's Big Boy and hand out tickets.

The show went on, and the King delivered what is considered to be one of his greatest performances.

Studio tours are offered. Call 818-840-4444 for more information.

Cholame

■ JAMES DEAN DEATH SITE

Near Highways 41 and 46, outside Cholame

James Dean got his last speeding ticket on the afternoon of September 30, 1955. He died in a car wreck later that day.

Take Interstate 5 north out of Los Angeles, then turn west on Highway 46. A memorial comes up in about thirty miles (right next door to a cafe). The actual crash site is about 900 yards up the road.

Fullerton

■ LEO FENDER FACTORY

Santa Fe and Pomona Streets, Fullerton

Leo Fender began tinkering with radios in grade school, and eventually graduated to public-address amplifiers, crude electric guitars, and amps. There's no agreement as to who designed the first real electric guitar (Les Paul, Ernest Tubb, and several others sometimes get the credit), but Fender made his place in pop history by being the first to effectively mass-produce electric guitars and amplifiers. Working with several collaborators at various locations, Fender created his first solid-body electric guitar (the Broadcaster, later renamed the Telecaster) in 1948, then produced the Fender Precision Bass (the first electric bass) in 1951 and the Stratocaster in 1954.

Leo Fender was born and lived his whole life in the Anaheim-Fullerton area, and was rarely seen without a pocket protector filled with pencils and a ruler. He sold the Fender company when he was in his sixties, but continued to design and manufacture guitars and was at his workbench until the day before he died in 1991, at age 82. Fender, who never learned to play guitar, was inducted into the Rock 'n' Roll Hall of Fame a few months after his death.

A plaque on the Pomona side of the Fullerton Transportation Parking Structure designates it as the "former site of the Leo Fender Factory for mass production of the Fender Fine Line Electric Instruments, 1945–1952," the time period that covers most of Fender's greatest achievements.

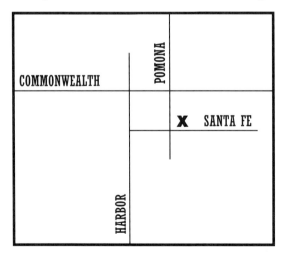

The Leo Fender plaque in Fullerton

Glendale

■ SAM COOKE'S GRAVE

Forest Lawn Cemetery, 1712 South Glendale Avenue, Glendale

Sam Cooke, the gospel singer who made pop history with "You Send Me," "Cupid," "Chain Gang," and a long list of other hits, is buried along the southeastern edge of Forest Lawn Cemetery, in what is known as the Court of Freedom. Cooke was killed in 1964 in the Hacienda Motel in south Los Angeles. His neighbors at Forest Lawn include Errol Flynn and Casey Stengel.

To get to the cemetery, take Highway 5 and exit east on Glendale Boulevard. Make a right at Forest, then a left at Glendale Avenue.

Joshua Tree

■ GRAM PARSONS CREMATION SITE

Joshua Tree National Monument

Gram Parsons worked with the Byrds, the Rolling Stones, and the Flying Burrito Brothers and was one of the inventors of country-rock. When Parsons died (from too much fast lane) in September 1973, his road manager hijacked his casket, brought it to Joshua Tree, and burned it, claiming that was what Gram would've wanted.

The cremation site, located near the Cap Rock formation (ask a ranger) is popular with Parsons cultists, but only the truly informed know that Parsons died at what was the Joshua Tree Motel on Highway 62, the main route into the park from Interstate 10. The motel is now the Copper Sands Youth Camp.

La Jolla

■ THE HARD ROCK CAFE

909 Prospect Street, La Jolla

In addition to the usual gold and platinum records and autographed photos and posters, the collection at the La Jolla Hard Rock includes a guitar signed by the original Ventures, one of John Densmore's snare drums from Doors days, one of Ringo Starr's snares from the Beatles' 1965 American tour, a 1960 Danelectro guitar signed by Duane Eddy, and a green velvet suit worn by Smokey Robinson on a 1965 tour.

The phone number is 619-454-5101.

Lancaster

■ ANTELOPE VALLEY HIGH SCHOOL

44900 North Division Street, Lancaster

Two of the all-time gym teacher's nightmares, Frank Zappa and Don Van Vliet (later known as Captain Beefheart), were fellow students at Antelope Valley High in the late Fifties.

To visit, take Interstate 14 north of Los Angeles. Lancaster is near Edwards Air Force Base.

Los Angeles

■ A & M

1416 North La Brea Avenue, Hollywood

In the Sixties, Herb Alpert and Jerry Moss converted Charlie Chaplin's film studio (built when Hollywood was young) into music-business landmark A & M. Of the countless recording sessions held on this site, the hugest probably came on the night of January 28, 1985, when the industry's stars gathered to make "We Are the World."

A considerably less bombastic project—but equally influential in its own way—was Joni Mitchell's *Blue*, recorded here in the winter and spring of 1970 and 1971.

■ AMIGO

11114 Cumpston Avenue, North Hollywood

Amigo recording studio operated from 1971 to 1991 and during those twenty years recorded everyone from Frank Sinatra to Poison, Christopher Cross to Van Halen, Seals and Crofts to Stevie Ray Vaughan. Metallica's *Master of Puppets*, Eric Clapton's *Behind the Sun*, Paul Simon's *Graceland*, and Randy Newman's *Sail Away* and "I Love L.A." are all Amigo products.

■ BLUE JAY WAY

Off Sunset Strip, Hollywood

George Harrison lived on Blue Jay Way in 1967. One day, Beatles publicist Derek Taylor attempted to visit but got lost in the fog. The song recounting the event became Harrison's contribution to *Magical Mystery Tour*.

Turn north on Sunset Plaza Drive off Sunset Boulevard. Continue north on Rising Glen when Sunset Plaza veers east. Turn left on Thrasher and follow it around toward the west; then turn north onto Blue Jay.

■ CAPITOL RECORDS

1750 North Vine, Hollywood

The thirteen-story Capitol Records tower opened in 1956 and immediately became an American icon. You know that the red beacon on the 87-foot rooftop spire blinks H-O-L-L-Y-W-O-O-D in Morse Code, and that the building (by architect Welton Becket) was not really designed to resemble a stack of records, right? What you probably don't know is that Capitol's recording studios are located not in the tower itself but in two big rooms in its base. Frank Sinatra cut some swinging sides here, way back when, and those sessions will probably stand as the studio's greatest.

Although the lobby is lined with gold records from rock 'n' roll's best—including the Beatles, Bob Seger, Pink Floyd, Steve Miller, and the Beach Boys—very little of the classic rock so commemorated was actually made on these premises. Still, most of those wonderful records were promoted by the workers lucky enough to toil inside Capitol's groovy tube, and that counts for something.

■ CHATEAU MARMONT HOTEL

8221 Sunset Boulevard, Hollywood

Jim Morrison lived—and John Belushi died—here. Renowned as a film-community favorite, the funky Chateau has housed Bob Dylan, Mick Jagger, various members of Led Zeppelin, John Lennon and Yoko Ono, and Gram Parsons. In August 1964, Barry Mann and Cynthia Weil wrote "You've Lost That Lovin' Feelin'" on a rented piano in room 2H at the Chateau.

The number to call to make your reservations is 213-656-1010.

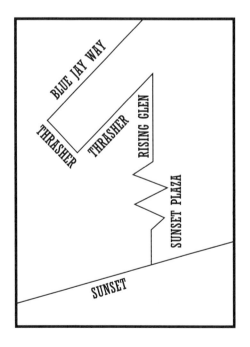

Blue Jay Way

■ CHEROKEE RECORDING STUDIO

751 North Fairfax Avenue, Hollywood

Cherokee's recording rooms have produced hits for Michael Jackson, Steely Dan, Rod Stewart, David Bowie, Alice Cooper, and Elton John.

■ THE CONTINENTAL HYATT

8401 Sunset Boulevard, Hollywood

During the Seventies and early Eighties, the Continental Hyatt was a major hostelry for touring and recording acts, a known favorite of Jefferson Starship, Led Zeppelin, Little Richard, and the Rolling Stones. In the Sixties, Jim Morrison was a regular guest, and drew a crowd along Sunset one day by hanging by his hands from his balcony railing. Hotel management, wary of the traffic-control problems such antics might create but careful not to offend a good customer, simply moved Morrison to a room facing away from the street.

The hotel is now called the Hyatt on Sunset, and the phone number for reservations is 213-656-1234.

■ THE EXECUTIVE ROOM

3953 Wilshire Boulevard, Los Angeles

In 1972, Billy Joel, discouraged by label hassles and probably embarrassed by his *Cold Spring Harbor* album (an error in mastering made Joel's voice sound somewhat chirpy), fled the East Coast to hide out in L.A. Under the name Bill Martin, he worked as a cocktail lounge pianist, and one of his known gigs was at the Executive Room. Joel eventually got a new record deal, and started climbing toward stardom again with the help of his first post-Executive Room release, *Piano Man.*

Today, like too many one-time L.A. landmarks, the Executive Room is no more. A shopping center stands at its former address.

565 Perugia Way, Bel Air

565 Perugia is the address of a house Elvis Presley leased for most of the Sixties. While the home you see here is not the one Presley lived in—that was torn down in 1990—you're looking at it anyway because on this site Elvis met the Beatles in August 1965. By all accounts it was an awkward occasion, with all of the King's entourage hovering around, but the Beatles did get him to loosen up enough to participate in a late-night jam session.

The site is in Bel Air, adjacent to the Bel Air Country Club.

■ GAZZARRI'S

9039 Sunset Boulevard, Hollywood

A big club, Gazzarri's has recently been popular with hard-rock fans. The phone number is 310-273-6606.

■ THE HACIENDA MOTEL

9137 South Figueroa Street, Los Angeles

On December 11, 1964, soul singer Sam Cooke met a woman named Elisa Boyer at a party uptown. The couple traveled to south central L.A. and registered at the Hacienda Motel as Mr. and Mrs. Cooke. Not long afterward, Cooke—wearing only a sport coat and his brogans—attempted to break in to the motel manager's room. Apparently Boyer had fled with the rest of Cooke's clothing, and he believed the manager, 55-year-old Bertha Franklin, was hiding her. Franklin shot Cooke three times with a .22 pistol and killed him.

The motel, located in a recently riot-torn part of town, is now called the Webb or the Polaris, depending on which side of the building you're standing. Neither name is listed in the phone book.

■ THE HARD ROCK CAFE

8600 Beverly Boulevard, Los Angeles

This Hard Rock Cafe is a tourist magnet, and the collection is impressive and ever-changing. Items here recently included two original tickets from the Beatles' last concert, a guitar from Bo Diddley, a single from the High Numbers (the Who, pre-Who), Rick Nelson and Elvis arrays, and a sequined Los Angeles Dodgers uniform worn by Elton John at a 1975 Dodger Stadium concert.

The phone number is 213-276-7605.

■ THE HOLLYWOOD BOWL

Highland Avenue and Cahuenga Terrace, Hollywood

The Hollywood Bowl, which bills itself as the largest natural amphitheater in the world, seats almost 18,000 and since its 1922 opening has been used primarily for summer concerts by the Los Angeles Philharmonic. But it serves in other ways, too—Hollywood High School uses the Bowl for commencement exercises, for example, and there's a lovely sunrise service every Easter.

All the jazz greats have played the Bowl, and so have quite a few notable rock acts. The Beatles performed here in August 1964 and 1965 and the tapes were later combined into *The Beatles at the Hollywood Bowl;* a Doors concert here became a big hit on the home video market in the Nineties.

The setting is sublime, the concerts continue. During the day, the grounds are open to the public and can be toured for free. Call 213-850-2000 for more information.

■ HOLLYWOOD SOUND RECORDERS

6367 Selma Avenue, Hollywood

The Coasters made records at Hollywood Sound, which should tell you how long it's been around.

■ THE HOLLYWOOD WALK OF FAME

Hollywood and Vine Streets, Hollywood

They don't just give away stars on the Walk of Fame—they sell them. The Walk's thrust is the movie business, of course, but rock 'n' roll has a decent representation. The Hollywood Chamber of Commerce (213-469-8311) sells a complete list of all the walk-of-fame stars for about $5.

■ MUSICIANS ON THE WALK OF FAME

Paula Abdul, 7021 Hollywood
Herb Alpert, 6929 Hollywood
The Beach Boys, 1500 Vine
The Bee Gees, 6845 Hollywood
Chuck Berry, 1777 Vine
Johnny Cash, 6320 Hollywood
Ray Charles, 6777 Hollywood
Crosby, Stills, and Nash, 6666
    Hollywood
Bobby Darin, 1735 Vine
Fats Domino, 6616 Hollywood
The Everly Brothers, 7000
    Hollywood
Fleetwood Mac, 6608 Hollywood
Aretha Franklin, 6920 Hollywood

Bill Haley, 6350 Hollywood
Jimi Hendrix, 6627 Hollywood
Michael Jackson, 6927 Hollywood
Elton John, 6915 Hollywood
John Lennon, 1750 Vine
Jerry Lee Lewis, 6631 Hollywood
The Monkees, 6675 Hollywood
Rick Nelson, 1515 Vine
Les Paul and Mary Ford, 1541 Vine
Elvis Presley, 6777 Hollywood
Little Richard, 6840 Hollywood
Smokey Robinson, 1500 Vine
Bob Seger, 1750 Vine
Ritchie Valens, 6733 Hollywood
Gene Vincent, 1751 Vine

■ THE LANDMARK HOTEL

7047 Franklin Avenue, Hollywood

Musicians visiting L.A. in the Sixties and Seventies could choose from three tiers of accommodations: acts new in town, either looking to secure a record deal or cut that first album, would stay at the Tropicana down on Santa Monica Boulevard. Next step up was the Continental Hyatt, and top of the line were the ritzy hotels in Beverly Hills.

Places like the Chateau Marmont, on Sunset, and the Landmark, a block

Janis Joplin's last home—The Landmark (Los Angeles)

north of Hollywood Boulevard, were for longer stays. For some rockers, one of the Landmark's attractions was its proximity to downtown-Hollywood drug dealers. Perhaps coincidentally, the hotel was one of Jim Morrison's favorites.

The Landmark is a *landmark*, though, because Janis Joplin was found dead in her room here on October 4, 1970. Her death was classified as an accidental overdose of heroin.

Since then, the Landmark has been known as the Highland Gardens Apartments and the Highland Gardens Hotel. Rooms now go for about $60 a night, and the phone number is 213-850-0536.

■ THE LOS ANGELES COLISEUM

3939 South Figueroa Street, Los Angeles

The Coliseum, a massive outdoor stadium, dates from 1923 and it's seen some memorable rock 'n' roll events.

In 1972 major soul performers staged Wattstax, a benefit extravaganza for the poor of the Watts neighborhood. Later, in the mid-Eighties, Bruce Springsteen's stand here drew more than 300,000 fans. (Those concerts were taped, and some of the songs ended up on his multi-disc live album.) It was also here at the Coliseum in 1982 that Prince opened for the Rolling Stones and was booed off the stage.

The Sports Arena next door was built in the late Fifties and is one of the busiest concert venues anywhere. Everyone's played the Arena—Ray Charles, Herman's Hermits, Otis Redding, Springsteen, Elvis Costello, U2, Billy Joel, Madonna, Michael Jackson. Pink Floyd first staged its in-concert version of *The Wall* here.

For upcoming events, call 213-747-7111.

■ THE LOS ANGELES FORUM

401 South Prairie Avenue, Los Angeles

In addition to being the home of the Los Angeles Lakers, the Forum's a popular concert site. One highlight: Bob Dylan and The Band taped most of their live album *Before the Flood* here in February 1974.

Call 310-673-1300 for more information.

6233 Hollywood Boulevard, Hollywood

One of the few concert spots to be mentioned in a Rickie Lee Jones song, the Pantages is best known for staging Broadway-style productions and as former home of the Academy Awards ceremony. The Talking Heads performances here were captured in the ebullient 1984 film *Stop Making Sense*.

Call 213-468-1700 to see what's playing.

Pickin' Up Good Vibrations

Brian Wilson recorded "Good Vibrations," his three-and-a-half-minute masterpiece, over a period of several weeks in 1966. He called seventeen separate recording sessions, used ninety hours of tape, and spent over $60,000—more money than most bands at the time would use up recording an entire album. Driven to compete with the Beatles' ever-more-creative records, and aiming to top his own Pet Sounds, *Wilson took the song to five studios, the elite of Hollywood's recording rooms. Cellos were taped at Sunset Sound Recorders; the opening vocal line and drum tracks were cut at Gold Star; Wilson did musical inserts at RCA and the hooky "I'm-pickin'-up-good-vibrations" vocal chorus at Columbia. The spacy theremin sounds were dubbed on at Western.*

Then, all the elements were blended into timeless pop. To revisit the golden age of the West Coast studios, just follow the "Good Vibrations" trail to CBS, Gold Star, RCA, Sunset Sound, and Western.

■ CBS

2120 Sunset Boulevard, Hollywood

2120 Sunset Boulevard had originally been the West Coast soundstage for CBS Radio, but in the Sixties it housed Columbia's recording studios. Tracks on Simon and Garfunkel's *Bridge Over Troubled Water* and the Byrds' *Sweetheart of the Rodeo* were recorded here.

Today, the building serves as studio space for CBS-owned radio and TV stations.

Phil Spector, the man who built the Wall of Sound (Gold Star Studios, Los Angeles)

■ GOLD STAR

6252 Santa Monica Boulevard, Hollywood

Part of Gold Star's allure for Brian Wilson stemmed from the fact that Wilson's idol, Phil Spector, built the Wall of Sound here. Spector-produced songs had an impressive track record in the Top Forty, but their influence carried far beyond their chart success. From the Beatles (Spector co-produced *Let It Be*) to Bruce Springsteen ("Born to Run" is an homage to Spector's sound), generations of musicians have come here to capture some of Spector's magic.

The studio started out in 1950 as an inexpensive place for songwriters to cut demos. In the late Fifties Spector discovered Gold Star's peculiar acoustics (which created a dense, echo-filled sound) and began to record hits here, beginning in 1958 with "To Know Him is to Love Him" by the Teddy Bears. Over the next few years, Spector produced "He's a Rebel" and "Da Doo Ron Ron" with various lineups of the Crystals, "Be My Baby" and "Baby, I Love You" with the Ronettes, "You've Lost That Lovin' Feelin'" with the Righteous Brothers, and the classic holiday album *A Christmas Gift for You*—all at Gold Star.

The main studio wasn't large, and never had air-conditioning. One hot night, according to legend, Tina Turner removed her blouse and recorded the vocal to "River Deep—Mountain High," the ultimate Wall of Sound expression, in her bra.

Spector perfected the Wall of Sound by layering band parts into dense backing tracks. The records were heavy on percussion, strings, massed vocal choruses, lots of echo, and the thundering tom-tom triplets of drummer Hal Blaine. When recording Beach Boys songs, Brian Wilson employed many of the same musicians Spector used on his sessions. For example, Blaine is the drummer-of-record on both "Be My Baby" and "Good Vibrations."

Gold Star sat on the southeast corner of Santa Monica and Vine. The building was razed by a shopping-center developer in the mid-Eighties.

■ RCA

6363 Sunset Boulevard, Hollywood

The RCA studios are at ground level on the west side of the Sunset Boulevard tower, which for years was RCA's West Coast headquarters. In addition to Brian Wilson, a long list of hitmakers worked in these rooms. Some highlights:

- Elvis Presley cut his movie soundtracks here, as well as his last hit, "Burning Love."
- The Jefferson Airplane recorded *Surrealistic Pillow* at RCA in the fall of 1966.
- In May 1965, Mick Jagger and Keith Richards wrote "Satisfaction" in Florida, cut preliminary tracks at Chess Studios in Chicago, and finished the song at RCA—all in the space of a few days. Other Stones songs recorded at RCA include "The Last Time," "Mother's Little Helper," "Get Off My Cloud," "Under My Thumb," "19th Nervous Breakdown," and "Paint It Black."
- RCA also was a favorite recording spot for the studio musicians who played on the Monkees' records. When it became known that the Monkees were only singing their songs, and not playing the instruments as their TV show depicted, a fake recording session was scheduled here for members of the press. As the TV stars demonstrated their true musical prowess to reporters and photographers in one studio, anonymous session men were cutting the real Monkees backing tracks down the hall.

The old RCA building is currently occupied by the German music giant Bertelsmann. The recording studios operate under the name Modern Sound, and keep busy recording TV sound effects. Many of the bleeps and squawks you hear on "Star Trek: The Next Generation" are made in the same studio where "Satisfaction" was mixed.

■ **SUNSET SOUND RECORDERS**
6650 Sunset Boulevard, Hollywood

When musician Tutti Camarata took over the original building at 6650 Sunset Boulevard in 1958, his principal client was Walt Disney, and most of the early Sunset products were soundtracks. Songs and background music for "The Wonderful World of Color," "The Mickey Mouse Club," *The Jungle Book,* and *Mary Poppins* were among Sunset Sound's successes, but by the mid-Sixties the world had turned to rock 'n' roll, and the studio followed.

In one frenzied week at Sunset in the summer of 1966 the Doors cut their entire debut album, which included "Break On Through (to the Other Side),"

"Light My Fire," and "The End." Prince recorded several *Purple Rain* tracks here in the summer of 1983, including "When Doves Cry." Sunset was also one of the Rolling Stones' favorite L.A. studios; they made *Beggars Banquet* here. A Sunset Sound recording engineer, Jim Messina, joined the Buffalo Springfield after working on one of their albums here. Later on, Messina met Kenny Loggins at Sunset.

■ SONGS RECORDED OR MIXED AT SUNSET SOUND

"Mr. Soul," The Buffalo
   Springfield
"Happy Together," The Turtles
"Last Train to Clarksville," The
   Monkees
"Do You Believe in Magic?" The
   Lovin' Spoonful
"Everyday People," Sly and the
   Family Stone
"I'll Be There," The Jackson 5
"(Theme From) Mission
   Impossible," Lalo Schifrin
"Me and Bobby McGee," Janis
   Joplin

"Fire and Rain," James Taylor
"Red Neck Friend," Jackson
   Browne
"Island Girl," Elton John
"Time Loves a Hero," Little Feat
"What a Fool Believes," The
   Doobie Brothers
"You Really Got Me," Van Halen
"1999," Prince
"Beat It," Michael Jackson
"The Glamorous Life," Sheila E.
"Manic Monday," The Bangles

■ WESTERN/UNITED
6000 Sunset Boulevard, Hollywood

The Western/United studios were designed by Bill Putnam in the mid-Fifties and quickly earned a reputation for having a large, "live" sound—perfect for recording the Beach Boys' soaring vocals. Putnam also built chambers at Western that produced superb echo effects without any electronic enhancement. Randy Newman (his *12 Songs* and *Sail Away* were recorded here), the Mamas and the Papas, Jan and Dean, Gary Lewis and the Playboys, and Johnny Rivers were among the many artists who honed the West Coast sound at Western.

Of all five "Good Vibrations" studios, Western was Brian Wilson's favorite.

Most of the Beach Boys' hits were made here, and for *Pet Sounds* alone the building has a place in history.

For most of its life, Western had a companion studio, United, down the street at 6050 Sunset. In 1978, studio owner Allen Sides began assembling the eight Western and United studios into one large complex, now called Ocean Way. Sides, a veteran engineer and collector of vintage microphones, has retained an impressive client list: Paula Abdul, Elvis Costello, Crowded House, Bob Dylan, Bruce Hornsby and the Range, Michael Jackson, Elton John, the Red Hot Chili Peppers, Madonna, Sinead O'Connor, Bonnie Raitt, Simply Red, Bruce Springsteen, Was (Not Was), and Wilson Phillips.

■ RADIO RECORDERS

7000 Santa Monica Boulevard, Hollywood

Founded in 1933 as a radio soundstage, Radio Recorders evolved first into one of the movie industry's favorite soundtrack facilities and then into a hot spot for swing and pop. Louis Armstrong recorded here, as did Nat "King" Cole, Duke Ellington, Ella Fitzgerald, Dizzy Gillespie, Woody Herman, Billie Holiday, Spike Jones, Ernie Kovacs, Gene Krupa, Charlie Parker, Oscar Peterson, Frank Sinatra, Art Tatum, Ben Webster, and Lester Young. A few of the classics produced here include "White Christmas"—the best-selling single ever—by Bing Crosby; "Jailhouse Rock," "All Shook Up," "Loving You," "Teddy Bear," "Return to Sender," "Treat Me Nice," and "I Can't Help Falling in Love With You" by Elvis Presley (who also recorded his first Christmas album at Radio Recorders during a heat wave in the summer of 1957); and "You Send Me" by Sam Cooke. In the early Eighties, part of the building functioned under the name Rock Steady Studio, and Patti LaBelle, Michael McDonald, the Temptations, Eddie Money, Cheap Trick, and X made records here.

The complex is now called Studio 56, and the client roster isn't slipping: the names range from Paula Abdul, C & C Music Factory, Color Me Badd, Dread Zeppelin, the Divinyls, Guns n' Roses, Martika, Ted Nugent, and Bonnie Raitt, to the Smithereens, George Thorogood, Was (Not Was), and Warren Zevon.

The Guitar Center, 7425 Sunset Boulevard, Hollywood

Since 1985, the Rock Walk has been the Mann's Chinese Theater for guitarists. The hand-prints-in-concrete treatment is not limited to guitar players, although many (Chuck Berry, Eddie Van Halen, Les Paul) are so honored. The display is in front of the Guitar Center, where the phone number is 213-874-1060.

■ THE ROXY

9009 Sunset Boulevard, Hollywood

For a couple of decades the comparatively tiny Roxy (capacity 400) was the top showcase club in town. Bob Marley's Roxy appearance in 1976, which made *Rolling Stone* magazine's list of the twenty best-ever concerts, and Bruce Springsteen's Roxy stand in 1978 (which resulted in a live radio broadcast, much bootlegging, and, ultimately, a few stellar cuts on Springsteen's live album) are perhaps the two most famous engagements. David Bowie and Prince, like so many other artists, played the Roxy en route to jobs in larger venues, and Pee-wee Herman was a cult phenomenon here before he went on to movie and television stardom. The Roxy was also home to *The Rocky Horror Show*—a live production, not the movie.

Upstairs is a private club called On the Rox, which reportedly remains a favorite hangout for entertainment-industry heavies. One such heavy, John Belushi, socialized at On the Rox on the night he died (in the Chateau Marmont Hotel down the street). An equally famous music-business watering hole, the Rainbow, is next door and was once Led Zeppelin's favorite place to get drunk in L.A.

The Roxy itself doesn't book acts anymore, but instead operates as a rental facility. Call 310-276-2222.

7317 Romaine Street, West Hollywood

As the Sixties turned to the Seventies, Motown czar Berry Gordy began to relocate his Detroit empire to the West Coast. He installed corporate headquarters in a high rise on Sunset Boulevard and sound studios at 7317 Romaine. Although some recording and mixing still went on back at Detroit's Hitsville U.S.A., the great late-period Motown songs were cut in California. Most of The Jackson 5's work was done at 7317 (also called Hitsville), including "ABC" and the dazzling "I Want You Back." Quite a few of the Temptations' later hits were also recorded here, including "Ball of Confusion" and "Papa Was a Rolling Stone."

The studio is now called Soundworks West and specializes in film soundtrack work (*Beauty and the Beast, Godfather III,* and *Grand Canyon* were scored here), but it also still books record dates. For example, Bruce Springsteen worked on his 1992 *Human Touch* at Soundworks.

■ THE TROPICANA MOTEL

8585 Santa Monica Boulevard, Hollywood

The Tropicana, long L.A.'s preeminent rock 'n' roll motel/dump, has been razed to make way for a Ramada Inn. During its run, the Trop was best known as home to Tom Waits.

For many years, record companies housed their up-and-coming rock acts here. Accordingly, things sometimes got quite rowdy. Next door to the Trop was Duke's, the best place on Earth to watch hungover rock stars eat breakfast. The Tropicana is long gone, and Duke's has relocated to a storefront next to the Whisky A-Go-Go on Sunset.

On the Trail of the Lizard King

These three locations, like about a hundred different places around Los Angeles, could legitimately post "Jim Morrison Slept Here" signs.

■ ALTA-CIENEGA MOTEL
1005 North La Cienega Avenue, West Hollywood

Jim Morrison occasionally kept a room at the Alta-Cienega, and it's possible, by staggering back and forth between this site and the next two while in a total stupor, to simulate a typical day in his life.

You can get a room here, too, for about $40 a night. The phone number is 310-652-5797.

■ BARNEY'S BEANERY
8447 Santa Monica Boulevard, West Hollywood

A major Morrison watering hole, also frequented by Janis Joplin and Alice Cooper, Barney's is still a good place to drink beer and eat beans till 2 A.M. Call 213-654-2287.

■ THE DOORS' OFFICE
8512 Santa Monica Boulevard, West Hollywood

The Doors' business office and clubhouse was located on the second floor of the small two-story building at 8512 Santa Monica Boulevard. On the ground floor was a rehearsal space and recording studio, where some of *L.A. Woman* was cut. Late in his life Jim Morrison was asked to record an antidrug public-service announcement for the Do It Now Foundation, and the taping session was held here, supervised by a foundation representative. Morrison got the

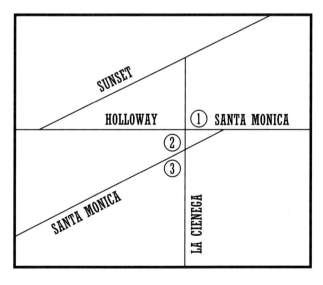

Jim Morrison
Country Safari:
1) Barney's Beanery
2) The Alta-Cienega Motel
3) The Doors office

"speed kills" part of the spiel right every time, but couldn't stop adding endorsements for just about every other kind of drug. Needless to say, the frazzled rep left without his PSA.

The businesses that have inhabited 8512 Santa Monica since Doors days don't always know its history. Recently, the first floor has been redone as a small cafe. A tourist was photographing the place one evening when a cafe worker approached, apparently confused. "Why do people take pictures here?" he asked.

■ THE TROUBADOUR

9081 Santa Monica Boulevard, Hollywood

The Troubadour has been a live-music hot spot for more than three decades. Favored by folk fans in earlier years and hard rockers lately, the room has witnessed such events as Elton John's American debut in August 1970—a concert *Rolling Stone* magazine considers to be one of the all-time greatest. It was at the Troubadour that Roger (then Jim) McGuinn met Gene Clark, and the two went on to form the Byrds. In 1974, a drunken John Lennon heckled the Smothers Brothers while they were performing here; as a result, Lennon was tossed out onto Santa Monica boulevard.

Between the launching of the Byrds and John Lennon's lost L.A. weekend, the Troubadour was the nexus for the Linda Ronstadt-Eagles-Jackson Browne country-rock movement.

And the beat goes on. The phone number is 310-276-6168.

■ T.T.G. RECORDING

1441 North McCadden Place, Los Angeles

Among many T.T.G. studio projects, three of the eleven cuts on *The Velvet Underground & Nico* were recorded here. So were the Band's last album and several Jimi Hendrix songs. The building now houses Shooting Star International, a talent agency for professional photographers.

■ VILLAGE RECORDER

1616 Butler Avenue, West Los Angeles

Steely Dan taped its first two records at Village Recorder, originally a three-room outfit that has since expanded to five. The Rolling Stones mixed *Goat's Head Soup,* Eric Clapton recorded his eponymous first solo album in 1970 (the jacket shows Eric standing on a ladder in Studio A), Bob Dylan and The Band made *Planet Waves,* Frank Zappa did *Joe's Garage I* and *II,* and the Beach Boys recorded "Sail On Sailor" here. Jim Morrison arrived on his twenty-seventh (and last) birthday, December 8, 1970, drunk, and sat down to recite and record some poetry. Fleetwood Mac used Village Recorder, too, and Robbie Robertson still keeps an office here.

■ WALLY HEIDER STUDIOS

Cahuenga and Selma Avenues, Hollywood

Wally Heider, a pioneer of mobile recording (he taped the Monterey Pop Festival and the Beatles' 1964 concerts at the Hollywood Bowl), later owned key studios in Los Angeles and San Francisco. His empire spanned a dozen different rooms and hundreds of hit records. Crosby, Stills, and Nash recorded "Marrakesh Express" and "Suite: Judy Blue Eyes" at Heider's L.A. location in the late Sixties; a decade later, Fleetwood Mac used the same rooms to cut parts of *Rumours.* T. Rex worked on its hugely influential *Electric Warrior* here.

Heider died in the late Eighties, and unfortunately his L.A. studios have, too.

■ WESTLAKE AUDIO

7265 Santa Monica Boulevard, 8447 Beverly Boulevard, Los Angeles

There are three studio rooms at Westlake's Santa Monica Boulevard address and a couple over on Beverly. A partial list of albums made here would include Michael Jackson's *Off the Wall, Thriller,* and *Bad,* Van Halen's second album, and Wilson Phillips' first.

8901 Sunset Boulevard, Hollywood

The Whisky is one of the world's most famous nightclubs. The Byrds, Cream, Jimi Hendrix, the Kinks, Led Zeppelin, Otis Redding, the Rolling Stones, the Talking Heads, the Who, Frank Zappa and the Mothers of Invention— it would be easier to list who *hasn't* played here.

One famous engagement was Johnny Rivers and his combo, who recorded a smash live album while employed as the house band. Then there were the Doors, who cemented their rock 'n' roll infamy in a summer-of-1966 stand. (Because of Jim Morrison's inebriated antics, the band was fired and rehired repeatedly that summer, and was banished for good after a performance of their naughty Oedipal opus, "The End." But by then it didn't matter—they'd signed their first record deal.) Another Whisky high/low: when Dennis Wilson was in his Charles Manson phase, the whole group would come here to party. Inevitably, Charlie's eerie aura—or maybe it was just his dancing— would clear the floor.

The Whisky's gone dark a few times, but through most of the Eighties and into the Nineties the club has stayed busy. Call 310-652-4202.

Mission Hills

San Fernando Mission Cemetery, 1160 Stranwood Avenue, Mission Hills

The San Fernando Mission has an old graveyard of thousands of pioneers. Richard Valenzuela, who died in an Iowa plane crash with Buddy Holly and the Big Bopper in 1959, is buried at Plot 247 of the mission's new cemetery, which is adjacent to the old one. His gravestone carries his real name and the words "Beloved Son & Brother." He shares the marker with his mother; on his side are etched the musical notes to "Come On—Let's Go" and on hers are the notes to "La Bamba." Actor William Frawley—Fred Mertz on "I Love Lucy"— is buried nearby.

Take the San Diego Freeway (405) to San Fernando Mission Boulevard, then turn left onto Stranwood.

The Whisky-a-Go-Go (Los Angeles)

Monterey

Monterey County Fairgrounds, Monterey

Monterey was the site of the first (and probably the best) of the big festivals. The event ran for three days in June 1967; admission ranged from $3 to $6.50 and attendance was estimated at about 50,000. The festival was billed as nonprofit, and the performers only got expense money—with the exception of Ravi Shankar, whose fee was $3,500. *Rolling Stone* magazine debuted a few months later with a where-the-money-went exposé.

Booths selling crafts, food, and various hippie paraphernalia crammed the grounds. The arena where the stage stood held only about 7,000, and many performers also played concerts on a "free" stage at Monterey Peninsula College.

The festival's board of governors reads like a who's who of rock musicians and producers: Lou Adler, Donovan, Mick Jagger, Paul McCartney, Roger McGuinn, Terry Melcher, Andrew Oldham, Alan Pariser, John Phillips, Johnny Rivers, Smokey Robinson, Abe Somer, and Brian Wilson. (It was Paul McCartney who got Jimi Hendrix and the Who included on the roster of performers.) The original idea had been to unite the musical "scenes" of Los Angeles and San Francisco, but the performers who really stole the show—like the Who, Hendrix, and Otis Redding—were outsiders and relative unknowns. In fact, many of the bands at the festival were new and didn't yet have record contracts. The Hunt Club, an enclosed bar and restaurant located just offstage, became a prime deal-making territory for competing record companies. (Also backstage, Bob Dylan manager Albert Grossman began badgering Fillmore founder Bill Graham to open a venue in New York City. Graham, with Grossman's backing, would soon open the Fillmore East.)

Neither the Rolling Stones nor the Monkees performed at the festival, but Brian Jones and Mickey Dolenz were in attendance (Jones introduced Jimi Hendrix's set). The Beach Boys were scheduled to play, but never showed. The whole event was documented in D. A. Pennebaker's film, *Monterey Pop*.

The fairgrounds haven't changed since 1967, and are open to the public during most business hours. To visit, take the Casa Verde exit off Highway 1

Jefferson Airplane at the Monterey Pop Festival—June 1967 (Monterey, California)

and follow the signs. The Monterey Jazz Festival is held on the grounds every September. Call 408-372-5863 for more information.

■ MONTEREY POP FESTIVAL PERFORMERS

The Association
Big Brother and the Holding
    Company
Mike Bloomfield and the Electric
    Flag
The Blues Project
Booker T. and the MGs
Buffalo Springfield
Eric Burdon
The Paul Butterfield Blues Band
The Byrds
Canned Heat
Country Joe and the Fish
The Grateful Dead
The Group With No Name
The Jimi Hendrix Experience
The Jefferson Airplane

Janis Joplin
Scott McKenzie
The Mamas and the Papas
Beverly Martin
Hugh Masekela
The Steve Miller Blues Band
Moby Grape
Laura Nyro
The Paupers
The Quicksilver Messenger
    Service
Lou Rawls
Otis Redding
Johnny Rivers
Ravi Shankar
Simon and Garfunkel
The Who

The Pacific Ocean

■ WEST

Janis Joplin died in 1970, and her ashes were scattered along the Marin County coastline by air. Nine years later, after the death of Little Feat leader Lowell George, his ashes were released from his fishing boat off the coast of Los Angeles.

When Beach Boy Dennis Wilson drowned in 1983, his widow and two of his former wives wanted a burial at sea—which is prohibited by federal law.

Finally, a special dispensation was obtained from President Reagan, and Wilson's body was taken out in a body bag and put overboard.

Pacific Palisades

■ **14400 SUNSET**

14400 Sunset Boulevard, Pacific Palisades

Dennis Wilson rented 14400 Sunset, set at the base of Will Rogers State Historic Park, in the late Sixties. Returning home from a recording session one morning in the spring of 1968, Wilson discovered that he had uninvited house guests—Charles Manson and his Family. (Wilson had befriended a couple of Manson's "girls" a few days before.) The Family stayed on for quite a while, primarily because Wilson and his drinking buddies enjoyed their orgies. Wilson also sponsored several recording sessions for Manson; in fact, the Beach Boys eventually put one of Manson's songs—"Cease to Exist," retitled "Never Learn Not to Love"—on their *20/20* album.

Wilson's relationship with his guest gradually soured ("sour" may be too gentle here—Manson actually pulled a knife on his host at one point), and after a long summer of supporting the dozen-plus Family members, Wilson just moved out, leaving the Family to be evicted by the house's owner. The Tate-LaBianca murders occurred about a year later.

Pasadena

■ **THE PASADENA CIVIC AUDITORIUM**

---

300 East Green Street, Pasadena

The big (almost 3,000 seats), beautiful (a $2 million renovation was recently completed) Pasadena Civic isn't often mentioned in lists of L.A. rock houses. Its usual fare is Emmy broadcasts, musical comedy productions, classical concerts, and organ recitals. But the theater took its place in rock 'n'

The house that Beach Boy Dennis Wilson briefly shared with Charles Manson (Los Angeles)

roll history in 1983 as the site of Motown's 25th anniversary television special *Motown 25: Yesterday, Today, Forever.* The event ran the gamut from great drama (Marvin Gaye's stoney lead-in to "What's Going On" and the Diana Ross-Mary Wilson tussle during the show's finale) to lame shtick (most of the comedy bits and Adam Ant's antics), but it's best remembered for Michael Jackson's electrifying performance of "Billie Jean." Jackson was headed for the top of the entertainment world before the special, of course, but his smouldering rendition (to a prerecorded backing track) and moon walk rank with rock 'n' roll's best TV moments.

For information, call 818-793-2122.

San Bernardino

■ **US FESTIVALS SITE**

Glen Helen Regional Park, San Bernardino

Backed by Apple Computer founder Steven Wozniak, the US concerts were the last ridiculously large rock festivals. Several hundred thousand people attended the two festival weekends (the first three-day event was in

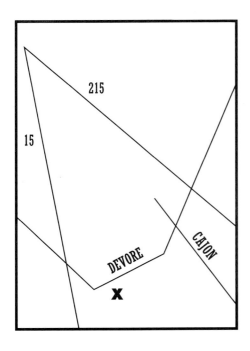

The US Festival site

September 1982, the second in May 1983). Ticket prices were in the $40 range—and Wozniak still lost $20 million. The talent (grouped on some nights by musical genre) was nonetheless quite impressive.

Performing at US '82 were Fleetwood Mac, Tom Petty, the Police, Jackson Browne, Pat Benatar, the Cars, Talking Heads, the Grateful Dead, the Kinks, the B-52s, Dave Edmunds, Santana, Eddie Money, Gang of Four, the Ramones, the English Beat, and Jerry Jeff Walker. The US '83 lineup included the Clash, Men at Work, Judas Priest, the Stray Cats, Ozzy Osborne, Scorpions, Missing Persons, U2, the Pretenders, Stevie Nicks, Van Halen, and David Bowie.

The Glen Helen Regional Park, a delightful place for fishing, hiking, swimming, and camping, is just off of Interstate 15 about an hour east of Los Angeles. The park is open from dawn till dusk every day, but some of the attractions are seasonal, and you should call ahead (714-880-2522). The US Festivals were held in the southeastern section of the park.

San Diego

■ CROCE'S

802 Fifth Avenue, San Diego

Opened by Jim Croce's widow Ingrid in 1983, Croce's has become a San Diego entertainment institution. The complex is in a historic section of downtown San Diego, and holds several restaurants and nightclubs—on some days, five different live bands can be found playing R & B and jazz. Also prominently featured is a large collection of Jim Croce memorabilia.

Croce's (or one of its surrounding affiliates) is open virtually round the clock. Call 619-233-4355 for more information.

Santa Monica

■ THE SANTA MONICA CIVIC AUDITORIUM

Main Street, near Pico, Santa Monica

The Santa Monica Civic Auditorium opened in June 1958 and has featured a variety of shows. Despite some early resistance to rock from the locals (an audience dress code—shirts and ties on boys, dresses or skirts for girls— was enforced at a 1966 Yardbirds concert), the hall became one of the L.A. area's premiere venues in the Seventies. Particularly memorable, it's been said, was David Bowie's *Spiders From Mars*-era engagement of October 1972.

But the Civic is important to rock primarily for one reason: it was the site of the Teenage Awards Music International (T.A.M.I.) Show in November 1964. That fabulous concert, which was filmed by Steve Binder for theatrical release, gathered Jan and Dean, Marvin Gaye, Chuck Berry, the Beach Boys, the Supremes, Smokey Robinson and the Miracles, the Rolling Stones, and James Brown for a once-in-a-lifetime bill. The movie is probably the single best document of James Brown's brilliance during that amazing epoch. His cape-shedding version of "Please, Please, Please" is unsurpassable.

The Civic has recently been undergoing renovation. Call 310-393-9961 for details.

Van Nuys

■ SOUND CITY STUDIO

15456 Cabrito Road, Van Nuys

Opened in 1969, Sound City Studio became popular with heavy-metal bands in the late Eighties and early Nineties—all or parts of hit albums by Poison and Nirvana were made here during that period. But the studio's reputation had been made much earlier, on projects by Tom Petty (with the Heart-breakers and, later, solo), Cheap Trick, REO Speedwagon, Foreigner, Elton John, George Harrison, Bob Dylan, the Tubes, Spirit, the Grateful Dead, Peter

Frampton, and Neil Young. The office walls now hold some forty platinum albums.

Two Sound City stories you'll want to tell at parties:

- Around Christmas 1974, Mick Fleetwood was shopping for a studio for Fleetwood Mac's next project. The band was in bad shape at the time, and Mick was looking to add some players. To demonstrate the control room's sonic capabilities, a Sound City engineer played Fleetwood a tape recently cut there by a duo named Buckingham-Nicks. As all students of pop history know, Lindsey Buckingham and Stevie Nicks were soon invited to join Fleetwood Mac, arriving just in time to participate in several enormous hits. (And, of course, both *Fleetwood Mac* and its follow-up, *Rumours*, were recorded at Sound City.)
- In 1968, Beach Boy drummer Dennis Wilson brought a pal named Charles Manson to Sound City to make some demos. Those sessions didn't turn out so well.

NORTHERN CALIFORNIA

Modesto

- ***AMERICAN GRAFFITI* INSPIRATION POINT**

Highway 99

Modesto is hometown to *American Graffiti* director George Lucas, and was his cruising ground as a youth.

Drive east from the San Francisco Bay area on Interstate 580 (be sure to look for historic Altamont Raceway, at the intersection of 580 and Interstate 5), then take Highway 205, then 120, then 99.

Oakland

■ ALTAMONT MOTOR SPEEDWAY

17001 Midway Road, outside Oakland

T he Rolling Stones' free concert at the Altamont Speedway on December 6, 1969, was a nightmare. About 300,000 fans showed up for the one-day event, several good bands played, only a few people died, and yet it's still considered one of the darker moments in hippie history. Here's why:

- The concert was originally scheduled for Golden Gate Park, then moved to the Sears Point Raceway. When the other venues backed out, the Speedway became home to the event hours before it was to begin.
- Santana opened the show at 10 A.M., and was followed by the Jefferson Airplane, the Flying Burrito Brothers, and Crosby, Stills, Nash, and Young. The Rolling Stones didn't start playing till after sundown.
- Doctors working the crowd had to send out for backup supplies of Thorazine, the drug then used to cool bad LSD trips.
- The Stones used the local Hell's Angels chapter as security at the Grateful Dead's suggestion. *Gimme Shelter,* the harrowing Stones-produced documentary of the tour, is full of footage of the Angels

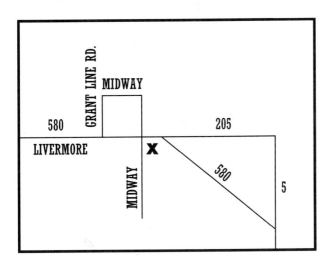

The Altamont Raceway

ABOVE: Hell's Angels "keeping the peace" at Altamont (outside Oakland, California)

RIGHT: Altamont today

keeping order by swinging sawed-off pool cues at spectators' heads. The Angels were paid for their services with $500 worth of beer.

- One of the Angels clobbered Jefferson Airplane lead singer Marty Balin—knocking him out—while the band was performing.
- Mick Jagger was another casualty. He got punched by a deranged fan as he arrived at the site.
- A spectator, eighteen-year-old Meredith Hunter, pulled a gun in front of the stage and was stabbed and stomped to death by the Angels while the Stones played. A legend has grown up that the band was performing "Sympathy for the Devil" at the time. In fact, the song was "Under My Thumb"—as anyone knows who's seen *Gimme Shelter,* which captured the murder on film.
- The racetrack infield was used as a landing area for helicopters during the concert. The stage and seating area were put in a ravine east of the track. Many fans came out to the site the night before the show and camped. It was 37 degrees when they woke up the next morning.
- The day-after coverage in the *San Francisco Examiner* also carried a story speculating that a Beatles breakup was imminent.

Now called the Altamont Raceway, the track has been functioning off and on since the Forties. Most recently it's been off, but plans are being made to reopen it for motorcycle and car racing. The site is about 45 miles east of Oakland. To reach the main entrance, take the Byron/Grant Line Road exit off Interstate 580, then bear back under the interstate onto Midway Road. The entrance is a paved road blocked by a line of concrete barriers and a wire gate.

Visitors should take note that the grounds are private property and not open to the public. The best and safest view of the concert area is from the southbound lanes of the I-580/I-5 interchange. It's a stunning sight. The miles of hills that surround the track are decorated with hundreds of huge power-generating windmills.

Palo Alto

■ PIGPEN'S GRAVE

Alta Mesa Cemetery, 695 Arastradero Road, Palo Alto

Ron "Pigpen" McKernan, a keyboardist and hard-living blues man, was an original member of the Grateful Dead. He died of liver trouble in March 1973, when he was 27. His grave marker says, "Pigpen was and is now forever one of the Grateful Dead."

The cemetery is next to the veterans' hospital between highways 101 and 280. Exit 280 at Page Mill Road and go east to Foothill Road, then south to Arastradero. Pigpen is in section 16 of the Hillview area, which is southeast of the main entrance. The hours are 8 A.M. to 6 P.M. Call 415-493-1041.

San Francisco

■ THE AVALON BALLROOM

1268 Sutter Street, San Francisco

One of the famed trippy San Francisco-sound ballrooms, the Avalon was the mid-Sixties booking domain of scenemaker Chet Helms. The Quicksilver Messenger Service played more than 75 shows here.

The Avalon is now the Regency II, a movie house. The phone number is 415-776-8054.

■ LEVI STRAUSS FACTORY AND MUSEUM

250 Valencia Street

The San Francisco Levi Strauss factory still makes 501s, and also has a small museum devoted to the company's history.

Free tours are conducted a couple of times every Wednesday. Call 415-565-9153.

Off Highway 101, San Francisco

Willie Mays played at Candlestick, and John Lennon did, too. This chilly big-league ball park was the site of the Beatles' last official public concert, which concluded their 1966 American tour. (The whole group would play together again in public only for the rooftop-concert sequence in *Let It Be*.) A stage was erected near second base for the August 29 show, and 25,000 fans attended. In what was, back then, a fairly standard-length concert, the band played twelve songs and left the stage after half an hour.

■ THE FILLMORE AUDITORIUM

1805 Geary Street, San Francisco

Promoter Bill Graham first used the Fillmore Auditorium in late 1965 to stage a benefit show for the San Francisco Mime Troupe. In January 1966, author Ken Kesey and a group of his cohorts, who called themselves the Merry Pranksters, held one of a series of outrageous Acid Tests here. The Tests set the mold for the San Francisco "scene" as we think of it: the Grateful Dead played, there was a psychedelic light show, and most of the participants took—or were dosed with—LSD. The venue's reputation had been made. For the next two and a half years, Graham booked the best of San Francisco's acts, as well as many major touring bands, into the auditorium. Though he eventually moved on to use the larger Winterland and Carousel ballrooms (the last Graham show at the Fillmore Auditorium was held in July 1968), the old theater at Geary Street remained close to his heart.

Graham restored the Fillmore Auditorium in the mid-Eighties, but the building suffered structural damage during the disastrous Bay Area earthquake of 1989 and has been closed ever since. According to a few lucky locals who saw the inside after the restoration, the job was beautiful; especially compelling was the collection of rock-show posters displayed in the balcony bar. At press time, Bill Graham Presents, the production company that survives its namesake (who died in a helicopter crash in 1991), plans to make repairs on the building and open it again as a concert facility.

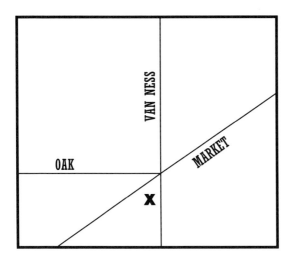

The old Fillmore West

■ **THE FILLMORE WEST**

1545 Market Street, San Francisco

After establishing his reputation by staging successful events at the original Fillmore Auditorium and the Winterland Ballroom, Bill Graham remade the Carousel Ballroom into a popular concert/happening/be-in facility in 1967. There was no fixed seating in the second-floor ballroom—which was about the size of a large high school gym—just plenty of open floor space for freeform dancing. The Fillmore West was one of the best concert halls in the world.

The two-story building, located on the corner of Market and Van Ness streets, now holds a Honda automobile dealership. The original Market Street entrance has been closed off, but the stairs to the second floor are intact from the Fillmore days. Hippie-era graffiti is still hidden among the building's nooks and crannies. Perhaps a Honda salesman will show you around.

■ **GOLDEN GATE PARK**

---

111 Eastshore Highway, San Francisco

The polo field at the western end of Golden Gate Park was the site of the first Human Be-In, a "Gathering of the Tribes," at which San Francisco acid-heads mingled with Berkeley radicals. Approximately 20,000 assembled on the field for the January 14, 1967, event. Entertainment was provided by the

Grateful Dead, Quicksilver Messenger Service, Big Brother and the Holding Company, and the Jefferson Airplane. The Be-In is significant to pop historians because it was the first major hippie event to get widespread attention in the straight media.

Eons later, in 1991, the field was the site of a memorial concert held for Bill Graham.

■ THE HARD ROCK CAFE

1699 Van Ness Street, San Francisco

As expected, San Francisco's Hard Rock is loaded down with gear relating to its home city—guitars used by Jefferson Airplane and Hot Tuna player Jorma Kaukonen, Huey Lewis' sunglasses, a snare drum signed by Creedence Clearwater Revival's stick man Doug Clifford, and a signed Rickenbacker guitar once owned by Roger McGuinn. Also on display is a collection of vintage hippie-era concert posters.

Call 415-885-1699 for more information.

■ LONGSHOREMAN'S HALL

400 North Point Street, San Francisco

A big round building near Fisherman's Wharf, Longshoreman's Hall has two claims to fame. First, it was the site in October 1965 of the original Family Dog rock dance, which featured music by the Great Society, the Charlatans, and the Jefferson Airplane. The dance was one of the very first blips on the hippie radar. Then, in January 1966, writer Ken Kesey and the Merry Pranksters brought a three-day Trips Festival—one of a series of traveling, LSD-fueled happenings—to the hall. The Trips Festival house band was, of course, the Grateful Dead.

The hall is located at Beach and Mason streets. It's within easy walking distance of Fisherman's Wharf, and has changed little since Prankster days.

■ THE MATRIX

3138 Fillmore Street, San Francisco

In his pre-Jefferson Airplane days, Marty Balin ran the Matrix, a mid-Sixties place for Bay Area folk folks. The Airplane had its very first jobs here.

The Matrix space is now occupied by a neighborhood bar called the Pierce Street Annex. Live music is played sometimes, but there's no reference made to the structure's acid-era heritage. Call 415-567-1400.

■ 746 BRANNAN

746 Brannan Street, San Francisco

Rolling Stone magazine's first office was on the second floor of 746 Brannan Street, which also housed a small print shop named Garrett Press. Rent was free, offered by Garrett in exchange for the magazine's printing business. *Rolling Stone*'s first issue included an investigative report on the Monterey Pop Festival (as mentioned above), an interview with Donovan, and a review (by magazine founder Jann Wenner) of John Lennon's acting in *How I Won the War*. It rolled off the downstairs presses on October 18, 1967.

The warehouse is in the area south of Market Street. After a couple of years, *Rolling Stone* moved to larger offices at 625 Third Street in the same neighborhood. Finally, in 1976, the magazine relocated to New York City.

■ 710 ASHBURY

710 Ashbury Street, San Francisco

In the hippie days, the Grateful Dead lived communally at 710 Ashbury. More items of tie-dyed apparel have been photographed in front of this structure than any other single location.

■ 2400 FULTON

2400 Fulton Street, San Francisco

2400 Fulton Street is a strange little mansion—in the Sixties, it was painted jet black with gold trim but it's now painted white—whose front yard is Golden Gate Park. For many years, the Jefferson Airplane used it as an office building/crash pad, and stories abound of wild parties and—believe it or not—ghosts.

■ WALLY HEIDER STUDIOS

245 Hyde Street, San Francisco

Wally Heider, of L.A. studio and mobile-recording fame, had the hottest studio in town in the late Sixties, and was among the first to document the San Francisco sound. Creedence Clearwater Revival recorded many songs here, as did Santana and the Grateful Dead.

The building still houses a recording outfit, called Hyde Street Studios.

■ WINTERLAND BALLROOM

Post and Steiner Streets, San Francisco

Impresario Bill Graham started booking concerts into the Winterland in March 1967, when some of his events outgrew the original Fillmore Auditorium. A few years later, Peter Frampton recorded most of his top-selling *Frampton Comes Alive!* album here.

Graham staged the final Winterland show—starring the New Riders of the Purple Sage, the Blues Brothers, and the Grateful Dead—on New Year's Eve 1978. The ballroom, which had originally been a venue for ice shows and boxing matches, was demolished in the mid-Eighties to make way for condominiums.

The Winterland lives on in history books as the site of two grand finales: both The Band and the Sex Pistols played their last live shows here. The Band's concluding notes came on Thanksgiving 1976. Filmmaker Martin Scorsese documented the concert, combining performance footage with interviews to

"The Last Waltz," Winterland—Thanksgiving 1976 (San Francisco)

make *The Last Waltz*. Bob Dylan, Eric Clapton, Ronnie Hawkins, Joni Mitchell, Van Morrison, Neil Young, and Muddy Waters provided guest-star highlights. A little more than a year later, on January 14, 1978, the Sex Pistols wrapped up their only American tour at Winterland. Not long after, lead singer Johnny Rotten announced he was leaving the group, and Sid Vicious O.D.ed.

Sausalito

■ THE RECORD PLANT

2200 Bridgeway, Sausalito

John Lennon and Yoko Ono attended the Record Plant's grand opening party on Halloween in 1972—they came dressed as trees. In the time since, numerous hits have been recorded here, including songs by Pablo Cruise, Jefferson Starship, Stevie Wonder, Sly Stone, and Huey Lewis. Fleetwood Mac worked on *Rumours* here, and John Fogerty cut *Centerfield*.

The studio is located just below the main part of Sausalito, in an area of old warehouses on the water. It's changed hands a few times and is now known as just the Plant. It remains a busy studio.

Westwood

■ ROY ORBISON'S GRAVE

Pierce Brothers Cemetery, 1218 Glendon Avenue, Westwood

Roy Orbison died on December 6, 1988, in Tennessee. He's buried in Pierce Brothers Cemetery, in an unmarked grave but in good company: Marilyn Monroe, Donna Reed, Natalie Wood, Minnie Riperton, and Buddy Rich are all here, too.

To get to Westwood, exit the San Diego Freeway at Wilshire Boulevard and drive east to Glendon Avenue.

HAWAII

Honolulu

■ THE HARD ROCK CAFE

1837 Kapiolani Boulevard, Honolulu

Like the other Hard Rock Cafes, the Honolulu outlet is a wildly popular place. The collection includes some unusual items: a Fender Jazz bass signed by Brian Wilson, a Jimmy Buffet array, a display honoring the Kau Kau Corner (the popular drive-in restaurant that once stood on this spot), and an impressive assembly of Brian Jones' personal effects.

Call 808-955-7383.

Lahaina

■ THE HARD ROCK CAFE

---

900 Front Street, Lahaina

Why does Hawaii get two Hard Rock Cafes? The collection in Lahaina includes the Abbey Road Studios harpsichord used in "All You Need Is Love" and "Lucy in the Sky With Diamonds," some of Roger McGuinn's "granny glasses" from the mid-Sixties, and a display of surfing trophies, posters, and gear.

Call 808-667-7400 for more information.

Pearl Harbor

■ USS ARIZONA MEMORIAL

Kewalo Basin, Pearl Harbor

Did you know that this memorial to the 1941 Japanese attack on Pearl Harbor was partially funded by an Elvis Presley concert in March 1961? Did you also know that it was Elvis' last concert (he played in the Navy base's Block Arena) for almost a decade?

The memorial is open every day except Monday, and the phone number is 808-422-0561.

OREGON

Eugene

■ UNIVERSITY OF OREGON

Off Interstate 5

Animal House, one of the greatest rock 'n' roll movies ever made, was shot at and around the University of Oregon. The food fight and the basement party, as well as the dead-horse and post-party-trial scenes, were all filmed in various hallowed halls on campus.

Lake Oswego

■ OUR LADY OF THE LAKE CHURCH

650 A Avenue, Lake Oswego

Bruce Springsteen married Julianne Philips at Our Lady of the Lake in May 1985. They were divorced in March 1989.

Portland

■ NORTHWEST RECORDERS

411 Southwest 13th Street, Portland

In 1963, the Kingsmen were making the circuit, playing in various clubs around the Northwest. One of their most popular numbers was "Louie Louie," an oldie written by Richard Berry. The group decided to tape the song and went to Northwest Recorders, where the entire session—including load-in and load-out—took one hour. Jack Ely, singer on the tune, left the Kingsmen right after that session and never sang with the group again.

A day or two after the Kingsmen recorded their version, Paul Revere and the Raiders, a Boise band that was also playing in the area, came to Northwest Recorders and cut the very same song.

The Kingsmen's rendition, meanwhile, was getting local air play, but didn't move nationally for several months. When it took off, though, it took off.

Soon after the "Louie Louie" sessions, Northwest's owner converted the studio into an optical lab and had the street address changed to 415. The building's second floor now houses a dance school; the first floor, which is where the studio was located, is empty. Most of the original Kingsmen still live in the Portland area, and three of them play oldies packages and the state fair circuit every summer.

WASHINGTON

Renton

■ JIMI HENDRIX'S GRAVE

Greenwood Memorial Park, 350 Monroe Avenue NE, Renton

Jimi Hendrix was laid to rest in Greenwood Memorial Park on October 1, 1970. His grave marker is a flat slab, etched with a drawing of an electric guitar and the inscription "Forever in Our Hearts."

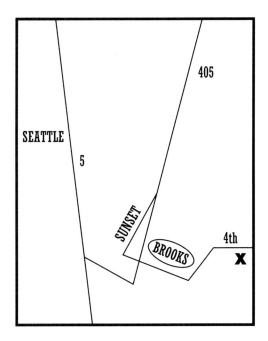

The Jimi Hendrix grave

The cemetery's phone number is 206-255-1511. To get there, take Interstate 405 south from the east side of Lake Washington. Exit on Northeast Sunset Boulevard in Renton; drive east on 3rd Street (also marked Brooks Road), then turn north onto 4th Street. The cemetery is on the right.

Hendrix's grave is in the rear section, near a large sundial. The cemetery is officially open during daylight hours, but locals say it's not unusual to see candles burning at the grave site late at night.

Seattle

■ **THE BLACK AND TAN CLUB**

1201 South Jackson Street, Seattle

Ray Charles moved to Seattle from Jacksonville, Florida, as a teenager. He started playing gigs around town, and the Black and Tan was one of the places where he performed in. Wong's Food Mart now stands at its address.

2411 Alaskan Way, Pier 67

Among rock 'n' roll's many infamous groupie tales, a real whopper took place at the Edgewater Inn.

Guests used to be able to fish out of the rooms here, and during a tour stopover in May 1969 Led Zeppelin members were reeling in women backstage and reeling in fish out their hotel window. One night things got boozy, then kinky, and according to the legend, a member of the band's entourage tied a female groupie to a bed and did lewd things to her with a shark (or a red snapper, depending on which version of the legend you believe).

The Edgewater is still at the water's edge, although fishing is no longer allowed. Call 206-728-7000 for reservations.

■ JIMI HENDRIX MEMORIAL

Woodland Park Zoo, Northeast 50th Street, Seattle

In the Eighties, a local radio station raised money for a memorial to native son Jimi Hendrix. The result was a bizarre but fitting structure in Woodland Park Zoo: a large, artificial rock that overlooks the zoo's African animals enclosure. A swirling—some might call it psychedelic—pattern of colored tile flows from the rock. The memorial's designer wired the rock with heating elements so that steam would rise from it whenever rain falls, and it's

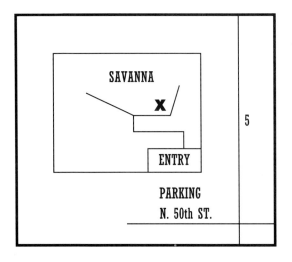

The Jimi Hendrix Memorial at Seattle's zoo

*ABOVE: Jimi Hendrix gravesite
(Seattle, Washington)*

*LEFT: The Jimi Hendrix memorial
at the Seattle Zoo*

surrounded by purple barberry bushes to achieve a "purple haze" effect. There's a small plaque at the site, but the zoo doesn't really publicize the memorial—and the heating elements have been broken for some time—so most visitors pass by the rock without ever knowing its purpose. Too bad.

There are three entrances to the zoo. The south entrance is closest to the memorial. To get there, exit Interstate 5 at Northeast 50th Street and drive west 1.3 miles. The memorial isn't far from the entrance. Admission is about $5; call 206-684-4800 for more information.

■ THE SOUND GARDEN SCULPTURE

7600 Sand Point Way NE, Seattle

Seattle was a hub for alternative bands in the late Eighties and early Nineties, spawning Nirvana, Soundgarden, Pearl Jam, and about twenty other groups. Soundgarden's namesake is a sculpture by artist Doug Hollis, an arrangement of large tubes that whistle and moan when the wind blows. The members of Soundgarden claim that the sculpture's sound wasn't their inspiration—they just liked the name.

The Sound Garden stands on the grounds of the National Oceanic and Atmospheric Administration, a few miles north of the University of Washington campus.

Bibliography

Books

Barth, Jack. *Roadside Hollywood.* Contemporary Books, 1991.

———. *Roadside Elvis.* Contemporary Books, 1991.

Bauldie, John. *Wanted Man: In Search of Bob Dylan.* Citadel Press, 1990.

Berry, Chuck. *Chuck Berry: The Autobiography.* Harmony Books, 1987.

Bird, Christiane. *The Jazz and Blues Lover's Guide to the U.S.* Addison Wesley Publishing, 1991.

Blaine, Hal, and Goggin, David. *Hal Blaine and the Wrecking Crew: The Story of the World's Most Recorded Musician.* Mix Books, 1990.

Bream, Jon. *Prince: Inside the Purple Reign.* Macmillan, 1984.

Bronson, Fred. *The Billboard Book of Number One Hits: The Inside Story Behind the Top of the Charts.* Billboard Publications, 1985.

Brown, James, and Bruce Tucker. *James Brown: The Godfather of Soul.* Thunder's Mouth Press, 1990.

Brown, Peter, and Steven Gaines. *The Love You Make: An Insider's Story of the Beatles.* McGraw-Hill, 1983.

Brown, Rodger Lyle. *Party Out of Bounds: The B-52's, R.E.M. and the Kids Who Rocked Athens, Georgia.* Plume, 1991.

Cantor, George. *Historic Landmarks of Black America.* Gale Research, 1991.

Charles, Ray, and David Ritz. *Brother Ray.* Dial Press, 1978.

Clark, Dick, and Richard Robinson. *Rock, Roll & Remember.* Crowell, 1976.

Clarke, Donald. *The Penguin Encyclopedia of Popular Music.* Viking, 1989.

Cotten, Lee. *All Shook Up: Elvis Day-by-Day, 1954-1977.* Pierian Press, 1985.

Crosby, David, and Carl Gottlieb. *Long Time Gone.* Dell Publishing, 1988.

Cross, Charles R. *Backstreets: Springsteen, the Man and His Music.* Harmony Books, 1989.

Culbertson, Judi, and Tom Randall. *Permanent Californians: An Illustrated Guide to the Cemeteries of California.* Chelsea Green Publishing, 1989.

Dannen, Fredric. *Hit Men: Power Brokers and Fast Money Inside the Music Business.* Vintage Books, 1991.

Davis, Sharon. *Motown: The History.* Guinness Publications, 1988.

Davis, Stephen. *Hammer of the Gods: The Led Zeppelin Saga.* Ballantine Books, 1989.

Draper, Robert. *Rolling Stone Magazine: The Uncensored History.* Doubleday, 1990.

Eliot, Marc. *Rockonomics: The Money Behind the Music.* Watts, 1989.

Elliott, Martin. *The Rolling Stones Complete Recording Sessions, 1963-1989.* Blandford, 1990.

Escott, Colin, and Martin Hawkins. *Good Rockin' Tonight: Sun Records and the Birth of Rock 'n' Roll.* St. Martin's Press, 1991.

Fein, Art. *The L.A. Musical History Tour: A Guide to the Rock and Roll Landmarks of Los Angeles.* Faber and Faber, 1990.

Fletcher, Tony. *Remarks: The Story of R.E.M.* Bantam Books, 1990.

Flippo, Chet. *Everybody Was Kung-Fu Dancing: Chronicles of the Lionized and the Notorious.* St. Martin's Press, 1991.

Fowler, Gene, and Bill Crawford. *Border Radio.* Texas Monthly Press, 1987.

Fong-Torres, Ben. *Hickory Wind: The Life and Times of Gram Parsons.* Pocket Books, 1991.

Fuqua, Christopher. *Music Fell on Alabama.* Honeysuckle Imprint, 1991.

Gaines, Steven. *Heroes and Villains: The True Story of the Beach Boys.* New American Library, 1986.

Gans, David, and Peter Simon. *Playing in the Band: An Oral and Visual History of the Grateful Dead.* St. Martin's Press, 1992.

George, Nelson. *Where Did Our Love Go? The Rise and Fall of the Motown Sound.* St. Martin's Press, 1985.

Gillett, Charlie. *The Sound of the City: The Rise of Rock and Roll.* Pantheon Books, 1970.

Goldrosen, John, and John Beecher. *Remembering Buddy: The Definitive Biography.* Penguin, 1987.

Guralnick, Peter. *Sweet Soul Music: Rhythm and Blues and the Southern Dream of Freedom.* Harper & Row, 1986.

Heylin, Clinton. *Bob Dylan: Behind the Shades.* Summit Books, 1991.

Hillburn, Robert. *Springsteen.* Rolling Stone Press, 1985.

Hirshey, Gerri. *Nowhere to Run: The Story of Soul Music.* Penguin Books, 1985.

Hopkins, Jerry. *Hit and Run: The Jimi Hendrix Story.* Perigee, 1983.

———— and Danny Sugerman. *No One Here Gets Out Alive.* Warner Books, 1980.

Lewisohn, Mark. *The Beatles Day-by-Day: A Chronology 1962-1989.* Harmony Books, 1989.

MacLean, Hugh, and Vernon Joynson. *An American Rock History, Part Two: Texas, Arizona and New Mexico.* Borderline Productions, 1990.

MacNeice, Jill. *A Guide to National Monuments and Historic Sites.* Prentice Hall, 1990.

Makower, Joel. *Woodstock: The Oral History.* Doubleday, 1989.

Marcus, Greil. *Mystery Train: Images of America in Rock 'n Roll Music.* E.P. Dutton, 1982.

Marsh, Dave. *Before I Get Old: The Story of the Who.* St. Martin's Press, 1983.

————. *Born to Run.* Dolphin Books, 1979.

————. *Elvis.* Thunder's Mouth Press, 1992.

————. *Glory Days: Bruce Springsteen in the 1980s.* Pantheon Books, 1987.

Merrill, Hugh. *The Blues Route.* William Morrow and Company, 1990.

Miller, Jim, ed. *The Rolling Stone Illustrated History of Rock & Roll.* Rolling Stone, 1980.

Miller, Terry. *Greenwich Village and How It Got That Way.* Crown Publishers, 1990.

Mitchell, Mitch, and John Platt. *Jimi Hendrix: Inside the Experience.* Harmony Books, 1990.

Monk, Noel E., and Jimmy Guterman. *Twelve Days on the Road: The Sex Pistols and America.* Morrow, 1990.

Palmer, Robert. *Deep Blues.* Penguin Books, 1981.

Pareles, Jon, and Patricia Romanowski, eds. *The Rolling Stone Encyclopedia of Rock & Roll.* Rolling Stone Press, 1983.

Presley, Priscilla Beaulieu, and Sandra Harmon. *Elvis and Me.* Putnam, 1985.

Pruter, Robert. *Chicago Soul.* University of Illinois Press, 1990.

Rayl, A. J. S. *Beatles '64: A Hard Day's Night in America.* Doubleday, 1989.

Rees, Dafydd, and Luke Crampton. *Rock Movers & Shakers.* Billboard Publications, 1991.

Scaduto, Anthony. *Bob Dylan.* Castle Books, 1971.

Shannon, Bob, and John Javna. *Behind the Hits.* Warner Books, 1986.

Smith, Richard R. *The History of Rickenbacker Guitars.* Centerstream, 1987.

Spector, Ronnie, and Vince Waldron. *Be My Baby.* Harmony Books, 1990.

Stambler, Irwin. *The Encyclopedia of Pop, Rock & Soul.* St. Martin's Press, 1989.

Staten, Vince. *Unauthorized America: A Travel Guide to the Places the Chamber of Commerce Won't Tell You About.* Harper & Row, 1990.

Stokes, Geoffrey, Ken Tucker, and Ed Ward. *Rock of Ages: The Rolling Stone History of Rock & Roll.* Rolling Stone Press/Prentice Hall, Inc., 1986.

Taylor, Derek. *It Was Twenty Years Ago Today: An Anniversary Celebration of 1967.* Fireside, 1987.

Tosches, Nick. *Unsung Heroes of Rock 'n' Roll.* Charles Scribner's Sons, 1984.

———. *Hellfire: The Jerry Lee Lewis Story.* Dell, 1982.

Turner, Tina, and Kurt Loder. *I, Tina.* William Morrow and Company, 1986.

Wheeler, Tom. *American Guitars: An Illustrated History.* Harper & Row, 1982.

Whitburn, Joel. *The Billboard Book of Top 40 Albums.* Billboard Publications, 1991.

———. *The Billboard Book of Top 40 Hits.* Billboard Publications, 1989.

White, Timothy. *Rock Lives: Profiles and Interviews.* Henry Holt and Company, 1990.

Wilson, Brian, and Todd Gold. *Wouldn't It Be Nice: My Own Story.* HarperCollins, 1991.

Wyman, Bill, and Ray Coleman. *Stone Alone: The Story of a Rock 'n' Roll Band.* Viking, 1990.

York, William, ed. *Who's Who in Rock Music.* Atomic Press, Seattle, 1978.

Articles

Aiges, Scott. "Hit Man." *The New Orleans Times-Picayune,* April 27, 1991.

Baker, Jackson. "A Memphis Life." *ElvisTown,* 1991-1992.

Bowman, Rob. "The Complete Stax/Volt Singles: 1959-1968." Box-set liner notes.

Bream, Jon. "Land of 10,000 Grooves: Three Decades of Minnesota Recording." *Minneapolis Star Tribune,* May 7, 1989.

Carlson, Tom. "Landmarks of the Early Years." *ElvisTown,* 1991-1992.

———. "At Home With the King." *ElvisTown,* 1991-1992.

Citron, Peter. "Grand Funk Tells About Chiquitas." *The Omaha World-Herald,* September 17, 1973.

Daley, Dan. "From Caruso to Hendrix: A Brief History of the New York Recording Scene." *Mix,* October 1989.

Day, Jeffrey. "Macon's Black Music Roots." *Macon Telegraph and News,* February 1, 1987.

Gordon, Robert. "The Devil's Work: The Plundering of Robert Johnson." *The LA Weekly,* July 5-July 11, 1991.

Hinckley, David. "Phil Spector: Back to Mono (1958-1969)." Box-set liner notes.

Hollreiser, Eric. "Rock of Ages." *New York,* February 6, 1989.

Jackson, Blair. "The Airplane House: Lore and Lunacy of San Francisco's Original Funky Chateau." *Bam,* December 1977.

LaVere, Stephen C. "Robert Johnson: The Complete Recordings." Box-set liner notes.

McLane, Daisann. "Lowell George, 1945-1979." *Rolling Stone,* August 9, 1979.

Montague, John. "The Norfolk Sound." *Oldies,* Spring 1990.

Nack, William. "Hey, Hey, Hey Good Bye!" *Sports Illustrated,* August 20, 1990.

O'Brien, Ron, and Andy McKaie. "Lynyrd Skynyrd: American by Birth (Southern by the Grace of God)." Box-set liner notes.

O'Neal, Jim. "Delta Blues Map Kit." Stackhouse/Delta Record Mart, Clarksdale, Mississippi.

Samuelson, Timothy. "Chess Records, 2120 Office and Studio—South Michigan Avenue: Preliminary Staff Summary of Information Submitted to the Commission on Chicago Landmarks." July 1989.

Santoro, Gene. "The House That Jimi Built." *Guitar World,* September 1985.

Selby, Gardner. "The Day Soul Cried: Dec. 10, 1967." *The Capital Times,* December 10, 1986.

Silverman, Richard. "Stax Recording and Production Studios: Request for Determination of Eligibility for Listing in the National Register of Historic Places." Prepared for Memphis Heritage, Inc., September 1989.

Skelley, Jack. "History in the Round." *California,* August 1991.

Smith, Richard R. "Early Fender History Re-examined." *Guitar Player,* December 1984.

Weatherford, Mike. "A Hard Day and Night: Beatles Concerts in Las Vegas Remembered." *The Las Vegas Review-Journal,* August 20, 1989.

Wheeler, Tom "Leo Fender: One of a Kind." *Guitar Player,* May 1978.

Whitall, Susan. "Rock Around the State: Take a Drive Into Michigan's Musical History." *The Detroit News,* March 22, 1991.

Willett, R. Martin. "Black Heritage, Macon, Georgia." Macon-Bibb County Convention and Visitors' Bureau.

"Driver of Car in Fatal Wreck Held for Manslaughter." *Delaware State News,* March 23, 1956.

"Gillsburg Plane Crash Kills Six." *The McComb Enterprise-Journal,* October 21, 1977.

"Live! Twenty Concerts That Changed Rock & Roll." *Rolling Stone,* June 4, 1987.

"Sigma Sound Studios." *Billboard,* September 16, 1978.

"The 100 Best Albums of the Last Twenty Years." *Rolling Stone*, August 27, 1987.

"The 100 Best Singles of the Last Twenty-five Years." *Rolling Stone,* September 8, 1988.

Index

USS Arizona Memorial [Pearl Harbor, HI], 237

Valens, Ritchie, 134–138, 214;
  gravesite of [Mission Hills, CA], 214
Van Nuys, CA, 223–224
Vaughan, Stevie Ray, 100, 158, 160, 171, 174
Vega, Suzanne, 12, 20
Velvet Underground, the, 19, 21, 36, 41, 212
Vicious, Sid, 25, 235
Village Barn, the [New York, NY], 34
Village Gate, the [New York, NY], 43
Village Recorder [West Los Angeles, CA], 213
VIP Club, the [Phoenix, AZ], 166
Violent Femmes, *161*
Virginia, 55

Waits, Tom, 38, 210
Walk of Fame [Philadelphia], 49
Walk of Stars [Austin, TX], 175
Wally Heider Studio [Hollywood, CA], 213
Wally Heider Studio [San Francisco], 233
Walsh, Joe, 158
Warhol, Andy, 36, 41
Washington (state), 238–242
Washington, DC, 55–57
Waters, Muddy, 20, 91, 93, 127, 235
Watkins Glen, NY, 44
Watkins Glen Raceway [Watkins Glen, NY], 44
Watt, James (former U.S. Secretary of the Interior), 55
Waxahachie, TX, 186–187
Welcome Center, the [Macon, GA], 85–86
"We're an American Band" (Grand Funk Railroad), 153–154
West Orange, NJ, 11

Westbury, NY, 45
Western/United [Los Angeles], 207–208
Westlake Audio [Los Angeles], 213
Westlawn Cemetery [Detroit, MI], 144
Westwood, CA, 235
WFIL [Philadelphia], 50–52, *51*
Whisky-a-Go-Go [Los Angeles], 214, *215*
Whitehaven, TN. *See* Memphis, TN.
Who, the, 13, 145, 154–155, 199, 216
WIBB Radio [Macon, GA], 86
Williams, Hank, 61, 62
Wilson World Hotel [Memphis, TN], 118
Wilson, Brian, 236
Wilson, Dennis, 214, 218–219, 224;
  Dennis Wilson/Charles Manson house [14400 Sunset Boulevard, Pacific Palisades, CA], 219, *220*
Wilson, Jackie, 7, 139, 144
Wilson, Kemmons, 110, 118
Wink, TX, 187
WINS Radio [New York, NY], 4, 157
Winterland Ballroom [San Francisco], 229, 230, 233–235, *234*
Wisconsin, 158–162
WJW Radio [Cleveland, OH], 156–157
"Wolfman Jack" (Bob Smith), 177, 178
Wonder, Stevie, 33, 83, 131, 142
Woodstock Music and Art Festival site [Bethel, NY], ix, 12–15;
  list of performers at Woodstock, 15
Woodstock, NY, 45
Wuxtry Records [Athens, GA], 80

York, PA, 53
Young, Neil, 19, 23, 46, 74, 158, 235

Zappa, Frank, 38, 57, 73, 194
  See also Mothers of Invention.
Zildjian Factory [Quincy, MA], 7
ZZ Top, 45, 91, 100, 176, 177, 180, 184